The Krays
Their Life and Crimes

By
Dan Shaw

They came from the tough streets of London's east end. They grew up together, they fought together, they ruled vast swathes of the city together, they murdered together, and together everyone considered them unstoppable. Ronnie and Reggie Krays reputation for violence preceded them wherever they went.

'The Krays' is the first in intended series of real life crime stories. Presented concisely, yet in detail, it tells the true story of the Krays, their murderous exploits and how they were finally brought to justice.

This book uses UK spelling

'The Krays' is the first instalment of the
'True Crime' series
By Dan Shaw.

Other books available are:

The Great Train Robbery

The Real Bank Job

ONE...DEAD MEN CAN'T SPEAK.

The Blind Beggar pub stands on Whitechapel Road. In the 1960s it was a typical east-end hostelry, frequented by typical east-end characters. The district of Whitechapel itself had no claim to fame other than being the location of the notorious 'Jack the Ripper' slayings. Now, almost eighty years after those horrific events, the memory of the Ripper killings had long passed into obscurity among the residents of the borough. Little did anyone know that Whitechapel was once again about to be visited by murder....

The Blind Beggar pub was quiet that mid-week evening. Aside from the barmaid, there were only four other people present. The old man divided his time by reading his newspaper and glancing at the television, and didn't take any obvious interest in the three men at the other end of the bar. Taking advantage of the lull in that evening's trade, the barmaid busied herself washing the glasses. It is possible that both the old man and the barmaid recognised one of the other patrons. If so, their instincts told them to steer clear, for George Cornell was not a man to be trifled with. He was an eminent hard man and professional criminal who plied his talents as a member of the infamous Richardson gang.

Cornell had seated himself on a barstool and was chatting casually to his companions. Even though he was in 'enemy territory' - the Kray twin's turf - he had little regard for the possible consequences. He made no secret of the fact that he wasn't afraid of the twins and their associates, and often openly issued insults about them. Perhaps the most famous of all his mockery was the occasion when he described Ronnie Kray as 'a fat poof'. No, George Cornell wasn't scared of the Krays; he wasn't scared of anyone and his presence was an unspoken statement of that fact.

When the door of the Blind Beggar opened, nobody took much notice. It would just be another punter in search of a drink. Unfortunately for the patrons, the new arrival wasn't just a punter looking for a drink. The figure in the doorway was another man whose notoriety preceded him. As Ronnie Kray and one of his henchmen strode into the pub, Cornell and his friends spotted them and, for Cornell at least, he still felt he had no reason to be apprehensive. After all, unlike many people who blustered from the sidelines, he meant everything he said.

A pistol suddenly appeared in the hand of Ronnie's henchman and he proceeded to fire two bullets into the ceiling. Within the confines of the bar the sudden noise was tremendous and while everyone else cleared the immediate area in sudden panic, Cornell stood his ground. After all, if Ronnie and his friend wanted a fight, then it would be churlish of him to refuse.....

"Well." Cornell smirked, as he watched Ronnie Kray approach. "Look who's here."
Ronnie made no reply; instead he halted only a few feet away and with his rival still staring him in the eyes, coolly pulled a 9mm pistol from his pocket, took aim then shot Cornell in the head.
Turning on his heel, Ronnie calmly left the pub. Meanwhile, Cornell's drinking buddies attended to their wounded friend.

Cornell would die in hospital a few hours later. The news of his death was received with elation by Ronnie Kray. He had made his first 'kill' and now would not be satisfied until his brother followed suit....

TWO...FORGED IN FIRE

Ronnie and Reggie Kray were born on the 24th of October 1933. The Kray family already consisted of a four-year-old boy, Charlie. The birth of the twins meant that finances - already stretched - would be placed under even more pressure. Despite this their mother, Violet, was overjoyed by the arrival of her two newest sons.

Money was always an issue for Violet, and in that respect she was no different to every other mother who lived in the east-end. Her husband, Charlie senior, didn't have a regular job; instead he made money by persuading people to sell unwanted clothes, jewellery and gold or silver, which he would then re-sell for a profit. His unusual vocation took him away from home for extended periods of time, leaving the bringing up of the three boys to Violet.

Life was hard for everyone in those days, and the Kray family was no exception. Living in Hoxton did them no favours, indeed, the area was so deprived that it was even looked down upon by impoverished people from neighbouring working class boroughs. Life may have been hard, but Violet made sure that her children never went hungry.

Despite being identical twins, it was obvious to all within their immediate circle of family and friends that Ronnie and Reggie were possessed of different personalities. Their individual characters formed at an early age and marked them out from one another, eventually even to those who didn't know them well. Most people regarded Reggie as the brighter of the two, and possessed of an outgoing nature. Ronnie, on the other hand, was quieter. He seemed to have difficulty communicating with people and would often express himself and his frustrations through bouts of anger.

Both boys were fiercely competitive, but their emulous nature was most in evidence when competing against each other. This rivalry was to prove a driving force which lasted throughout much of their lives. During their childhood, a great deal of the mutual competition centred on their attempts to win favour with their mother. Despite Violet's strict approach that she show no partiality to any of her boys, Ronnie and Reggie would each go out of their way to attempt to influence her into favouring them just that little bit more than the other twin.

Paradoxically, whilst being the greatest of rivals, Ronnie and Reggie were always fiercely loyal to each other. If someone wished to cause trouble for Ronnie, then Reggie would be duty bound to step in and help. Conversely, if Reggie was ever threatened then he could absolutely rely on Ronnie to provide assistance. This underpinning bond of blood and east-end values was to later ensure that the Kray twins became unstoppable within the London underworld.

Shortly before the outbreak of World War Two, the Kray family escaped the deprivation of Hoxton, swapping it for another solidly working-class, yet better area. There were no pangs of sentiment as they packed up their belongings and made the move to Bethnal Green, taking up residence in a small terraced house among a row of identical properties on a street called Vallance Road.

Soon the horrors of war were visited upon the capital. The air force of Hitler's Nazi Germany began to make regular large scale bombing sorties over the east-end of London. Thus began the blitz. As well as concentrating their offensive upon the strategically important docks and industrial areas of the city, the Luftwaffe considered the civilian population as legitimate targets for attack. Many tens of thousands of people were killed, injured and rendered homeless as a result of the Luftwaffe's aerial offensive, while huge swathes of the capital were laid waste by high explosive and incendiary bombs.

Fearing for the safety of her sons, Violet moved Charlie, Ronnie and Reggie to rural Suffolk. Despite being safe from the ravages of the blitz, Violet soon found herself to be desperately homesick, so it wasn't long before she moved the family back to Vallance Road.

During this time Charlie senior, the Krays oft absent father, had been called up for military service. Charlie didn't much care for the idea of army life, and the prospect of dying for a cause in which he had little interest enamoured him even less. Taking the decision to ignore the call to arms, Charlie went on the run. He continued with his buying and selling as if nothing had changed, using his extensive network of contacts to evade the police. Though still largely removed from family life, he would sometimes risk his liberty by visiting Vallance Road to see Violet and the boys.

Charlie senior had every reason to be careful, because he was indeed a marked man. The police and military were after him and the former would often turn up unannounced at Vallance Road in search of this elusive absentee. Ronnie and Reggie sometimes witnessed the raids upon their home as the police attempted to capture their father. The routine was always the same, the police would push their way past Violet, who'd be angrily ranting at them, and quickly search the property in the hope of finding her husband. On two occasions Charlie senior was actually present when the police suddenly appeared.

The first time the police came calling, the Kray family was taken by surprise. Charlie senior barely escaped being caught and hid beneath the dining table, shielded from view by the large tablecloth which covered it. While their father cowered under the table, Ronnie and Reggie were questioned as to his whereabouts. They knew nothing. They hadn't seen their father in months. They had received no letters or had any other communication with him. The twins had been told that the police would be intercepting all mail bound for 178 Vallance Road in the hope of picking up some intelligence which may lead them to Charlie senior. The officers present knew they had told the truth about not getting any mail, so they were probably telling the truth about not having seen their father. Satisfied, the police left. As Charlie emerged from beneath the tablecloth, the Kray family enjoyed a good laugh at the expense of the Metropolitan Police.

The second time the police mounted a raid on the Kray's home while Charlie senior was visiting he was again caught on the hop, diving into the stair cupboard just as the police were entering the house. After conducting a search of the upstairs, one of the policemen lingered in the hall while his colleagues went through the rest of the house. Suddenly, inexplicably, his interest was piqued by the sight of the cupboard. Striding forwards with arm outstretched he was about to grab for the handle and look inside.

"You don't think my dad would be hiding in there, do you?" Ronnie said sarcastically, just as the policeman reached the door.

The policeman agreed. It was a stupid place to hide. He went off to search elsewhere. After the police had left, Charlie senior emerged from his hiding place. It was the closest of close shaves. Had it not been for Ronnie's quick thinking he would have been frogmarched away to prison then the army. Once again the house reverberated with the sound of laughter....

It was during these formative years that both boys discovered a liking for violence. They would fist fight with anyone who chose to take them on, and always be there to provide physical support for one another should it be required. It is likely that the tales told to them by their maternal grandfather, John Lee, inspired that taste for physical confrontation.

Granddad Lee was a well known old time east-end character, who once made his living as a bare-knuckle fighter. 'Cannonball', as granddad Lee was known, would often regale the twins with stories of his fights. Even as an old man, Cannonball liked to keep himself in shape, and would regularly work out on the improvised punch bag which hung in his back yard.

While London had been ravaged by the German bombing campaign, nowhere had been hit harder than the east-end and it was among the ruins of bombed and burned out buildings that Ronnie and Reggie Kray began to make their mark.

Fighting was the norm among boys and more often than not no excuse was needed to initiate it. That said most confrontations were about reputation or the control of territory. Boys would form themselves into gangs and invade neighbouring areas (which may be only a street or two away) to assert their authority. Boys from the area subject to such invasions were duty bound to defend their 'turf'. While there was never a shortage of boys willing to pitch in with these battles, there were a few who immediately began to stand out from the crowd as a result of their physical prowess and naked aggression. It was against this backdrop that Ronnie and Reggie rapidly cemented a reputation as skilled and fearless fist fighters. Such was their status that they became well known and feared by not only those in the immediate area but within the gangs farther afield. Of course, with that burgeoning reputation came the obligatory challenges from other 'hard nuts' who wanted to take the Krays down a peg or two. Both Ronnie and Reggie were never ones to refuse an invitation to prove who the best fighter in the street or the area was. They took on and beat all comers, and this only helped to enhance their own stature in the rough and tumble world of east-end youth.

While the twin's talents for street fighting was obvious, it was their elder brother, Charlie, who saw that the skills they had acquired on the streets of Bethnal Green could be honed and turned into something which might give them a way out of the east-end. Unlike his father, Charlie junior had not shirked his wartime responsibilities. Enlisting with the Royal Navy, Charlie had soon established his own reputation as a gifted boxer. It was during a period of home leave that Charlie decided to pass on some of his newly found skills to his younger brothers. He rigged up an improvised punch bag and set about coaching the boys.

Given their obvious talent for street fighting, it was perhaps understandable that Ronnie and Reggie easily took to boxing. From the off, Charlie could see that the pair displayed a flair for the sport. He was convinced that they could make a name for themselves within the tough world of boxing and that it would prove their ticket to a better life.

During a visit to a local fair, the twins happened upon the boxing booth. Such an attraction was usual in the fairgrounds of those days. It was a simple scenario; members of the audience would be challenged to fight a professional boxer. Anyone up for the challenge would be invited to step into the ring and, should they survive the allotted number of rounds, they would win a few pounds in prize money. Perhaps not to be expected, when called upon to do so, no-one in the audience wanted to accept the offer of a bout with one particularly hardened fighter. Suddenly a lone voice called out from the crowd. It was Ronnie Kray. He'd fight the professional. Everyone laughed when they saw the skinny youth who had accepted the challenge. The master of ceremonies declined the offer, saying that he was not big enough to tackle the pro. When asked by Ronnie if there was someone else he could fight, the ringmaster informed him there was no-one in his stable of boxers small enough to fight the boy. To the crowds' surprise, Reggie piped up. He'd fight his brother. Accompanied by the cheers of the crowd, the pair was waved into the ring and, after donning the gloves, commenced to attack each other. Just three rounds later the bout was stopped and the twins were paid a few shillings for their trouble. Such was their performance in the ring, that a local coach who had witnessed the fight approached the pair, offering to train and mentor them.

Ronnie and Reggie eagerly subscribed to their new regime. They trained regularly and made sure they followed the raft of instructions given to them by their coach and it wasn't long before they were beginning to win fight after fight.

Of the pair, Reggie showed the most promise. While Ronnie would wade into his opponents and overwhelm them with a combination of brute force and aggression, Reggie displayed more finesse and practical ability. Indeed his skill and technical approach were such that they led him to be crowned schoolboy boxing champion 1948.

Despite both exhibiting great potential as boxers,

the twins could never control their violent tendencies. The fights inside the ring were never enough to quench their thirst for ungovernable brutality. Much to the dismay of those who were schooling them in the art of boxing, they continued to fight on the streets whenever the opportunity arose. Here they weren't constrained by the rules of the ring, they could punch and kick and head butt to their hearts content. It was during one such street fighting incident that the twins were first brought to the attention of the authorities.

Ronnie and Reggie had been accused of beating up a sixteen-year-old boy. The attack was witnessed by couple of bystanders who reported what they had seen to the police. This evidence, along with a complaint by the victim, was enough to see Ronnie and Reggie remanded in custody. They were due to stand trial for the assault at the Old Bailey and all involved were sure the pair would be sentenced to a lengthy term in prison. However, before the case reached the court, both witnesses and the victim himself suddenly retracted their statements. When the case was finally heard, it was dismissed through lack of evidence. The twins walked free. That the victim and witnesses for the prosecution had refused to continue with the case was no co-incidence. They had been given warning by persons unknown (who no doubt were street gang friends of the twins) that to pursue the matter would lead to serious consequences for them and their families.

For Ronnie and Reggie, they learned an important life lesson. They now knew they could manipulate the system by threat of violence....

It was only a year later when the twins found themselves charged with another serious assault. This time, it looked as if there was no way out of their predicament.

It all started when the twins were standing outside a local cafe. They were minding their own business when a policeman approached from behind and pushed Ronnie in the back. The constable had hardly time to order the pair to move along when Ronnie wheeled and punched him in the mouth. As the officer was falling to the pavement, the twins made good their escape. This escape proved short lived, as within the hour Ronnie had been arrested. For the sake of family honour as much as his wish to get revenge on the constable whom Ronnie had struck, Reggie let his temper get the better of him. He returned to the area where he knew the police officer in question would be patrolling and hunted him down. Approaching from behind, Reggie tapped the constable on the shoulder. As he turned, a vengeful Reggie delivered a stunning straight right to the policeman's jaw.

Reggie was quickly arrested and a few days later hauled, along with Ronnie, before the local magistrates. The twins silently acknowledged that there was little they could do to influence the outcome of the trial, and were both expecting to be handed jail terms as a result. In a last ditch attempt to garner a measure of leniency, they had enlisted the help of a local priest. The priest turned up at court and made an impassioned plea to the presiding magistrate. To the twin's amazement, the rouse worked, and despite the odds, while they were indeed found guilty their punishment was nothing more than a period of probation.

There remained one seemingly insurmountable obstacle between Ronnie and Reggie and whatever career they wished to pursue. In early 1952, the twins received their call up papers. As with all young men of the time, upon reaching the age of eighteen, they were required by law to undertake two years military service. Though they displayed the same enthusiasm for army life as their father, the twins reported for duty with the Royal Fusiliers at the Tower of London. These two most unlikely of recruits were only a matter of hours into their new career when they decided they had had enough of army life. It was pointless to stay here, they agreed. They weren't going to let anyone shout orders or make them do things which they didn't want to, they might as well just go home. They announced their decision to the other recruits who looked on dumbfounded as they packed their cases and headed for the exit. On their way out they were stopped by an irate NCO who demanded to know where they were going.

"Home." They replied as one. "To see our mother."

Unfortunately this was not reason enough for the army to allow them unofficial leave. The corporal who had interdicted them took hold of Ronnie's arm with the intent of halting his progress. Before he really knew what had happened, the unfortunate NCO found himself on the receiving end of a punch from Reggie. No sooner than the unconscious corporal had hit the floor, the twins left the barracks and made for Vallance Road.

The following morning the army came for them. The twins made no fuss and returned quietly to the Tower where they were promptly sentenced to seven days close confinement in the guardroom.

Upon their arrival at the guardroom, Ronnie and Reggie met up with another prisoner. Like them, Dickie Morgan was a most reluctant recruit. He had spent time in borstal and didn't take kindly to authority. Almost immediately, the trio agreed that they would go absent without leave as soon as the opportunity to do so arose. They were released from custody at the same time and almost immediately left the barracks and headed for Dickie's home.

While managing to evade the attentions of the police and military authorities, Dickie introduced the twins to his own world. A world where crime was the accepted way of earning a living. It was within this world of nightclubs, shady deals and easy money that the twin's eyes were opened to all manner of possibilities. For tough men such as them, surely it would be simplicity itself to forge a lucrative career within the criminal underworld of London?

By the time the army finally caught up with them the die had been cast. Ronnie and Reggie's future would not be one which included prize fighting, or indeed any other form of gainful employment. They were determined to make their own mark on the world, stamping their authority in the exciting and dangerous world of organised villainy.

The remainder of their time with the military was no less colourful. When they were eventually caught, they divided their time between civilian and military prison. These experiences only served to further cement the twins blossoming criminal ambitions as, during their sentences, they were introduced to a wide range of hardened miscreants from across the country. Their new friends were all too eager to provide tuition to the twins on how to conduct all manner of illegal enterprises.

A year later, when their last sentence was complete, Ronnie and Reggie were dishonourably discharged. They returned home to Vallance Road and set quickly about adding meat to the bones of their plans to make a living from crime....

THREE...SPHERE OF INFLUENCE.

Unemployed and with nothing much to occupy their time, Ronnie and Reggie took to frequenting a local snooker hall. The Regal had long seen better days, but its potential to generate an income did not go unnoticed by the pair. Although once a popular venue where young men gathered to play the game, the snooker hall found itself beset with problems. Local gangs would congregate there to conduct their fights. Vandalism of the tables and other fixtures was rife, and as a result what was left of the Regal's regular patrons were finally driven away. Having seen enough of the disorder, the club's manager resigned. With no-one else willing to take on the role, Ronnie and Reggie presented themselves to the owner. Their proposal was simple; they offered to rent the Regal for £5 a week. The proposition was accepted and the twins duly became the proprietors.

The twins immediately took over the Regal and all the trouble which plagued the place came to an abrupt end. Everyone in the area knew the twins and word had gone out that people causing trouble at the club would have to answer to Ronnie and

Reggie. Tough nuts though most of the Regal's rabble-rousers were, none of them fancied the idea of finding themselves on the receiving end of the twin's wrath.

The club was quickly decorated and a gaggle of second-hand snooker tables brought in. Order restored, the Regal soon began to return a tidy profit.

Aside from providing easy money, the Regal also gave the twins a base from which they could conduct future operations.

At this point in time, Ronnie and Reggie were not well known among the wider criminal fraternity. To this end, and once it was known that it was making money, there were various attempts to muscle in on the Regal's action. A Maltese gang appeared in the club one day to demand protection money. They may have heard something of the nature of these two young twins, but cared little about it. Unfortunately for the Maltese mobsters, as far as Ronnie and Reggie were concerned, the lack of respect was mutual.

The gang informed the twins that they would take their first payment immediately then return for more cash each week thereafter. If it wasn't forthcoming the Regal would be trashed and its customers driven off. Should Ronnie and Reggie wish to resist, then they would find themselves with enforced hospital stays.

Via a contact, Ronnie and Reggie had been

forewarned of the Maltese gang's intentions. They both knew that everything they had worked for up to this point in time would be washed down the drain should they allow themselves to be extorted. If their reputation went, the game would be well and truly up. Both quickly realised that, instead of a stumbling block, any success against the gang would put the names of the Krays on the lips of a wider audience, so it was up to them to make the most of the coming battle. It was also important that they were seen to be acting as a pair, with no support from their friends and fellow street thugs. After all, they concluded, anyone can be tough when they are mob handed; to be tough when the odds are stacked against you is what separates the men from the boys....

When the mobsters arrived at the club they quickly set about intimidating those inside. It was a show of force designed to impress upon the young managers that they - the gang - were to be taken seriously. As the gang members were making their presence known the twins appeared from the back office and confronted them.

Outnumbered and knowing they were squaring up to hardened gangsters, the twins had taken the precaution of arming themselves with long and especially sharpened rifle bayonets. The racketeers must have wondered about the sanity of the two young men who were choosing to take them on.

That they had seen fit to confront the gang members in the first place was a sleight which could not be ignored, but to do so while carrying weapons?! The upstarts would have to be taught a lesson they would not easily forget.

A few words of warning were ignored by the twins. If, Ronnie and Reggie said, the mobsters wanted the Regal, they would have to take it by force, going through them to get to the cashbox.

In the ensuing fight, things quickly went awry for the would be extortionists. After a furiously savage locking of horns in which the bayonets were used to devastating effect, the Maltese gangsters were made to turn tail and run, dragging their wounded away with them.

While word was slowly beginning to spread about the Kray twins, it was the incident with the Maltese gang which finally brought their names to the attention of the east-end underworld.

Business remained brisk at the Regal and the snooker tables were turning over a tidy profit. However, a tidy profit would never be enough to slake the thirst for power and money which the twins had developed.

Their growing reputation meant that ne'er-do-well's began to gravitate towards the club in the hope of associating themselves with the Krays. Soon the twins had recruited a useful cadre of hard men and an outer circle of cohorts who would readily collaborate in any of their schemes.

Ronnie and Reggie were quick to realise the potential of their fledgling gang and how it could be put to use to expand the 'business'. There was no finesse about their enterprise, after all, first and foremost the twins were fighters and so not naturally inclined to conduct their affairs with any degree of tact.

Ronnie in particular was always keen to make sure that his and Reggie's names were synonymous with violence. He would gather his followers at the Regal to announce that they were to go off on a raid. He and Reggie, accompanied by their cronies would head out to a local pub, dance hall or club. Once inside they would instigate a fight. Fixtures and fittings would be smashed and the male patrons attacked and beaten. Their work done, the gang would return to the Regal or go onto another place where the same thing would happen. Although it might appear to be just mindless violence, there was method contained within it. The twins had a reputation, but it was vital that they maintain and expand that reputation if they were to climb the greasy pole and advance in the brutal environment which was the London organised crime scene.

It didn't take long for the mention of the Krays name to strike fear into the hearts of those landlords and club owners who heard it. This fear was then carefully translated into action as the twins set about extorting money from them and other local businesses. For a weekly fee, pubs, clubs, shops, restaurants, bookmakers, illegal gambling joints and any other place of business could buy themselves protection from rival gangs. If they paid they were free to carry on trading, if they refused or defaulted, then a group of men would descend upon their establishment to destroy everything they could get their hands on.

While their criminal enterprises were returning good profits, the Kray twins were still operating on a local level. It was a small pond, and certainly not big enough for the two fish that swam in it. The twins concluded that they needed to break out of the east-end, but how were they to do it? Anyone who had associations with the underworld knew there were two main organised crime syndicates operating in the west-end of London. Now, they agreed, was the time to reach out....

Although not planned, Ronnie and Reggie's timing could not have been better. The two main players on the west-end crime scene were both old timers. Between them, Billy Hill and Jack 'Spot' Comer had overseen their own long standing criminal empires. They controlled everything from gambling and prostitution, to drinking and protection. The two men had operated with the minimum of animosity for over a decade, and at one point had briefly joined forces to oust the then ruling White crime family from the highly lucrative west-end nightclub scene. Though Spot and Hill worked together when events required, recently things had turned sour. Following his release from prison after serving time for his part in a failed £1.25 million (£31.5 million in 2018 terms) robbery attempt on Heathrow airport which was masterminded by Spot, it wasn't long before another daring – but this time successful – heist hit the national headlines. A post office van containing £200,000 (almost £5.8 million in 2018 terms) was robbed. Although there was never any proof to link him with the robbery, it was widely acknowledged that Billy Hill had been behind the raid. As a result, Hill's reputation was given a boost and he was thereafter regarded as the number one gangster in London. Spot became increasingly jealous of Hill's success. To add insult to injury for Spot, the notorious Italian Sabini gang (whose operations Spot and Hill had largely taken over after a brief but deadly gang war) had re-grouped and were looking to recover their interests in the horse racing scene.

The animosity between Spot and Hill simmered until Hill finally decided that Jack Spot must be dealt with once and for all. Ordering a few of his henchmen, including 'Mad' Frankie Fraser to carry out the job, Spot was attacked and badly cut across the face. It was after surviving this savage assault that Spot decided if he was to successfully counter the threat which Billy Hill and, latterly, the Sabini's posed, he needed to draft in some extra muscle. Casting his net wide, Spot was soon made aware of the two young brothers from Bethnal Green and invited Ronnie and Reggie to meet him. Jack Spot was impressed by the twins and immediately engaged their services.

The twins knew that acting as Spot's minders would provide them with a useful lever upon which they could gain entry into a new and highly lucrative marketplace. They took to their new role with typical gusto, relishing the promise of serious violence which accompanied it.

Without delay Ronnie and Reggie began to make preparations for an all out assault upon Jack Spot's rivals. Using Vallance Road as their headquarters, they prepared men and assembled weapons.

It wasn't long before a scrap of information found its way to 'Fort Vallance'. Some of Jack Spot's enemies were meeting in a pub in Islington, North London. This was just the opportunity the twins had been waiting for. If they acted quickly they would have a lot of Spot's rivals all in one basket. A shock raid by them and their underlings against the pub could see this opposition wiped out in a single bloody action. The word went out to the Kray gang members and, after assembling at the Regal, weapons were issued and the attackers set out for Islington. Their arrival at the target pub proved a bitter disappointment for all concerned, but especially Ronnie. Instead of catching a gang of villains by surprise and meting out punishment, Kray style, on behalf of Jack Spot, they burst into an empty pub. The twins weren't to know that Billy Hill had got wind of the attack and ordered his men to leave. The decision to pull out his own troops was one which Hill had not taken lightly, yet one for which he had very good reason. Like Jack Spot, Hill was a seasoned gangster. He didn't operate by use of violence, but principally through the threat of violence. He had many hard men among his own gang – including the notorious 'Mad' Frankie Fraser. Fraser's own reputation for brutality preceded him wherever he went and he was feared by everyone, including the underworld's toughest characters.

It wasn't that Billy Hill was scared, but that he knew a large scale fight, conducted in public by rival criminal gangs, would bring much unwanted police attention upon him and his operations. In simple terms it would damage his rackets and cost him money, so it made sense to lay low and deal with Spot and his two new minders another time.

Stung by the failure of the Islington job and with their lust for violence unquenched, the twins weren't about to let matters rest. They quickly identified another venue in which they could satisfy themselves. It had nothing to do with Spot or Hill, but everything to do with the twin's need to place their names on the lips of every criminal gang in London....

It was just another night in the little social club on Clerkenwell Road. There was nothing out of the ordinary about the place, save for the fact that it was home to a small time Italian gang whom the twins presumed to be associates of the Sabini's. Just after 10pm, Ronnie Kray walked into the club. Nobody took much notice until he challenged those inside to a fight. In response a bottle was thrown at Reggie's head. It missed. He repeated his challenge, but no-one reacted. Pulling out a semi-automatic pistol, Ronnie fired three shots into the wall. Still, there was no response. Frustrated, Ronnie turned and walked out. By using a gun in the headquarters of another gang, Ronnie had made a statement which could not be ignored. The Krays meant business, and to underestimate them was a mistake which nobody should make....

In the days when most criminals throughout Great Britain shied away from firearms, Ronnie was never adverse to their use. About the same time as the failed Islington job, the twins were informed that there was trouble on their own territory. A car dealer who paid protection money to the twins informed them that a customer was demanding a refund for a car he had purchased. The car dealer refused, so the man said he would return with some of his friends to get by force the £120 owed to him.

Knowing that it was necessary to make it known that those paying protection money to the Krays would indeed be protected from such threats, but more excited by the prospect of a confrontation, Ronnie armed himself with a pistol and set off to the car dealer's pitch to lay in wait for the customer and his friends. When the man returned he was alone. He had decided to keep the car. Ronnie blanched with anger at being denied his chance to fight and vented his frustration by shooting the man in the leg.

As had become standard practice, the wounded customer was visited in hospital by some anonymous man who persuaded him not to pursue the matter with the police. If he failed to comply there would be serious consequences for both him and his family. Needless to say, the victim suddenly developed amnesia and could tell the police nothing of substance about the incident....

FOUR...PARTNERS IN CRIME.

While the Kray twin's predisposition for extreme violence continued, their approach served to isolate them from the very people with whom they were attempting to court favour. Tiring of life in the underworld, Jack Spot retired and turned his attentions to running a furniture business. Spot's departure left the Krays friendless. Friendless they may have been, but they were determined not to withdraw from the money making potential which the west-end offered.

Eventually, the opportunity they had been awaiting presented itself.

The owner of a west end club called The Stragglers approached the twins and asked for their help. He wanted them to stop the incessant fighting which was blighting his bar and driving legitimate customers away. This was the 'in' Ronnie and Reggie had been looking for. They quickly took over responsibility for the security of The Stragglers and soon had the club returned to normal. Using the club as their forward operating base, the twins knew they could begin to extend their influence to all points of the compass.

Things seemed to be going well for Ronnie and Reggie, they had not only managed to secure a foothold in the west-end of London, but their various enterprises in Bethnal Green and the surrounding areas were generating sizeable amounts of cash. Unfortunately for them, things were about to change...

After having become embroiled in a dispute between the owner of The Stragglers and a local Irish gang, Ronnie decided that the latter should be taught a lesson. The moral of the story was to be as simple as it was brutal; mess with the Krays or anyone associated with the Krays, and you will be removed from the scene with extreme prejudice. Taking a small team of his most trusted accomplices, Ronnie led a raid upon a pub which the Irish gang used as their headquarters. The pub was empty of the gang apart from one man who was unfortunate enough to be in the wrong place at the wrong time. Enraged that another opportunity for a gang fight had eluded him, Ronnie subjected the man to a savage beating which was so brutal that it almost cost him his life.

Ronnie was subsequently arrested and charged with inflicting grievous bodily harm. He was later found guilty of the offence and sentenced to three years imprisonment.

With Ronnie away, Reggie was allowed to manage their business affairs without constant interference from his brother. Ronnie's incessant demands that rivalry or insult should be met with savage retribution had served only to hold them back. Perhaps, just perhaps, they had accrued enough of a reputation to dispense with the continual need for violence? Surely by now, the mention of their names was enough to stop people from interfering in their affairs?

Reggie opened his own club. The Double R stood on the Bow Road. With much effort, Reggie soon turned it into the busiest nightclub in the east-end. Although much of his energies were taken up with the Double R, the west-end was not to escape the attention of Reggie. Quietly, far more subtly than Ronnie would ever have allowed, Reggie expanded the Kray's interests. He moved into protecting illegal gambling dens in Mayfair and Belgravia. These high rolling affairs attracted persons of standing and made their organisers vast profits. The money associated with these operations meant they were prime targets for extortion and robbery. The people running the dens could hire their own muscle, but they were no match for the hardened criminal gangs who predated upon them. By bringing in Reggie, they were not only buying physical protection, they were buying the peace of mind that no-one would be foolish enough to interfere with something which was associated with the name Kray.

While business under Reggie's directorship continued to flourish, Ronnie's time in prison was less profitable. While he had started off well enough his physical presence, reputation and violent tendencies meant he ruled quickly the roost, controlling the inmate's scams and the trade in prison tobacco (which was the accepted currency). Upon his transfer to the Isle of Wight, ironically for good behaviour, things quite quickly spiralled out of his control. Isolated from his friends and family, Ronnie's mental health began to deteriorate. This deterioration was accelerated when Ronnie was given news of the death of his favourite aunt.

Ronnie was quickly certified as insane then moved to a psychiatric hospital in Surrey. Unlike prison, this place seemed not to pay too much heed to security. It was a flaw which Reggie quickly identified. During his weekly visits, Reggie could see visible improvement in his brother, but he knew that Ronnie would be held at this place indefinitely so long as the authorities regarded him as insane. It was a caveat which was unacceptable to the twins, and they soon began to conspire in an effort to make sure Ronnie's stay would be as brief as possible.

The fact that they were identical twins had worked in their favour on many occasions. When one of them hit somebody it was always difficult for the police to prove if the perpetrator was Ronnie or Reggie. On more than one occasion this confusion, and the inability to prove guilt beyond reasonable doubt as to which one was responsible, had resulted in Ronnie and Reggie walking free from court. Now, Reggie determined, if they could only pull off a subtle variation of the same stunt again....

As with all good strategies, the escape plan was simple. During his weekly visit, Reggie presented himself at the usual time, though on this occasion he attended the hospital wearing a distinctive light-coloured overcoat. He chatted easily with the guards as he was going through the visitor screening process, one or two of them even passing compliments about his smart overcoat. Once inside, the twins met and innocently began passing the time with idle chit chat. While appearing relaxed, the twins were awaiting their chance to put Reggie's plan into effect.

Eventually the moment arrived. The man watching over the visitors was momentarily distracted. Seizing his opportunity, Ronnie pulled on the overcoat and walked out of the room. Saying his goodbyes to the guards, he left the hospital and made his way to a waiting car. It wasn't until the end of visiting time that the attendant realised that the man sitting quietly before him was Reggie. The police were called and Reggie was questioned about his brother's disappearance. Reggie was adamant. He thought that his brother had gone to the toilet and was simply awaiting his return. He hadn't noticed - as the attendant also hadn't noticed - that his new coat had gone missing. There was nothing the police could do, so Reggie was released. By this time Ronnie was safely ensconced in a caravan deep in rural Suffolk.

Despite the best efforts of the police, Reggie ensured that Ronnie remained free until after his certification of insanity had expired. He then accompanied him to the police station where he was removed to Wandsworth prison to complete his sentence.

Being back with his old cellmates and with access to regular visits from his family and friends ensured that Ronnie's condition remained as stable as anyone could hope for.

When Ronnie was released, he stepped back onboard a ship which he barely recognised. Reggie had done wonders with the business, transforming it from a motley collection of scams into a highly profitable enterprise. Money was no object and Ronnie was quick to enjoy the good life which had eluded him these past few years.

Much to the chagrin of some in 'the firm' (as the Kray gang was now known) Ronnie's return spelled the end of this quiet period. Over the past three years, led by Reggie, they had discreetly got on with empire building. But doing things the quiet way was never Ronnie's forte, so he soon began to plan battles with rival outfits – outfits who posed no threat to the twins or their wider business operations. Ronnie had no regard that such missions would detract from what should have been the focus of their business (making money), or bring upon them the unwanted attentions of the police. As far as he was concerned, instead of Reggie's comparative low key approach, the best way to ensure future expansion was through the use of violence.

Ronnie and Reggie's difference of opinion was plain to see by those close to them, and it must be recorded that the vast majority of the firm favoured Reggie's approach. Tensions between the pair as to the direction of their enterprise could not be resolved and only caused to further hinder the opportunities which were opening themselves up to the Krays.

Despite the clash of wills, it was around this time that the twins undertook what was to prove their biggest and most profitable business undertaking....

Esmeralda's Barn was a fashionable and successful casino. Situated in the heart of Belgravia, one of the most affluent districts in London, it was frequented by the wealthy, the titled and the famous. One day, in the autumn of 1960, the majority shareholder was paid an unannounced visit by Ronnie and Reggie and their financial advisor, a man by the name of Leslie Payne. Allowing Payne to do much of the talking, the twins sat back and glared at the man they had come to see. Payne's proposal was simple. The man would agree to sell his controlling share in Esmeralda's to Ronnie and Reggie and be paid £1000 (£24,500 in 2018 terms) for his trouble. The sight of the twins scowling at him across the desk, along with his knowledge of their reputation, was enough for the man to agree. At a stroke, Ronnie and Reggie had bought themselves into the very heart of the west end club scene....

The new decade ushered in a new era for the Krays and their firm. Their business concerns and criminal enterprises were bringing in handsome dividends, but the jewel in the crown was Esmeralda's. The casino was a veritable licence to print money. Each week it took around £1500 (in excess of £32,000 in 2018 values) on the gambling tables alone.

It was during this time, when they had gained the notoriety they craved amongst other underworld figures throughout the capital and indeed beyond, that Ronnie allowed his 'secret' to become public knowledge. During their ascent up the slippery pole to gangland power, it would have been little short of professional suicide for Ronnie to admit that he was a practising homosexual. That he had always surrounded himself with good looking young men was explained away with the excuse that they were his errand boys, there to fetch and carry or to listen out for gossip which they would then report. Now, with the firm embedded in both the west and east ends of London, Ronnie saw little reason to cover up his sexuality. The news slowly seeped out and caused consternation among some (homosexuality was a criminal offence in those days), acknowledgement of suspicions by others and derision by the twin's rivals. Ronnie seemed to care little of what others thought; he just went ahead and did his own thing, taking young men to dinner or away for weekends in the country....

Tales of Ronnie's sexuality even made it to the national press when, in July 1964, the 'Sunday Mirror' ran a front page exposé detailing his relationship with a then unnamed Lord of the realm. The headline read 'THE PEER AND THE GANGSTER: YARD INQUIRY'. The article inferred that Ronnie and a certain conservative peer were engaged in a homosexual affair, and this was being investigated by the Metropolitan Police. At a time when such sexual practice was illegal in Britain, the story could have easily meant the end of Lord Robert Boothby's political career. That Boothby was bisexual there was no doubt, but whether or not his relationship with Ronnie entered into the physical is still cause for conjecture. What is clear is that Boothby was having an affair with renowned cat burglar Leslie Holt, and it was through Holt that Boothby was introduced to Ronnie Kray. Ronnie's own motives were quite straightforward, if he could strike up a relationship with the powerful and extremely well connected Boothby, then the latter's influence could be of use to the twins should they ever find themselves in serious trouble with the authorities. Ronnie was keen to oblige Lord Boothby by supplying him with a string of handsome young men and organising homosexual orgies in which the Lord was a willing participant. In return, Boothby granted Ronnie small personal favours. The arrangement suited Ronnie, he would continue to let his new friend have his fun, but one day he would have to repay all the 'kindness' by helping the twins escape whatever fate the authorities may have in store for them.

The story rumbled on and at one point it seemed that the country was about to witness a major scandal. During this time Ronnie was named as the gangster but Boothby's name was kept out of the press, that was until The Times printed an open letter from Lord Boothby stating that he was the other man in the article. He went on to explain that while he had indeed met a gentleman who was at that time unknown to him, the man had simply proposed a business venture which Boothby turned down. Only later, Boothby claimed, did he become aware that the gentleman in question was Ronnie Kray.

With nothing but hearsay on their side, the owners of the Sunday Mirror were forced to print an unconditional apology and paid Boothby £40000 (£768000 in 2018 terms) compensation.

Despite the glare of publicity surrounding Ronnie's dealings with Boothby and an ongoing media interest in their criminal enterprises, the twins did not rest on their laurels. They continued to open their own clubs, or buy into established ones.

In spring 1962 they opened The Kentucky, in Stepney. The Kentucky soon became a success and – like the twins other ventures – began to return a healthy profit. Not long afterwards they bought a share of The Cambridge Rooms on the Kingston bypass.

Celebrity seemed now to be stalking the Krays. Through their clubs they were rubbing shoulders with many celebrities of the day. Photographic records of Ronnie and Reggie with stars of film and TV, sporting bigwigs and pop singers attest to the fact that they were moving in circles which only a few years previously, would have been deemed impossible.

Throughout the first half of the 1960s, in what was seen by many as the high water mark of the Kray's criminal career, their empire continued to expand. Despite their success, the twins were beginning to find it difficult to capitalise upon their many business interests. Rather than interference from the authorities or rival gangs, this issue was self-inflicted. Their focus was on expansion, but while in the process of acquiring new concerns, they began to neglect their existing ones. Esmeralda's Barn – the place which always turned a handsome profit – began to run at a loss and eventually closed down, while the Double R had its licence revoked.

The failure of their business ventures never seemed to worry the twins, it was almost is if they had become bored with their existing interests and were only interested acquiring new ones.

Money, or the generation of it, also seemed not to figure too highly on the twins list of priorities. To them status and reputation was always more important than profits. While allowing their business interests to fray at the edges, both Ronnie and Reggie's attention was elsewhere; focused on grandiose schemes which were often too outrageous to be taken seriously. It appears that Ronnie led the way in this particular field, dreaming up outlandish ideas for businesses which had no hope of success. One of the most memorable of the twin's crop of investments was a plan to build a new town in Nigeria. Introduced to the scheme by Ernest Shinwell, the son of the famous Labour politician Manny Shinwell, the twins immediately invested £25000 (£465000 in 2018 terms) into the project.

Other large sums followed, but the project stalled and the money vanished.

It was around this time that the Krays attempted to establish contact with the American Mafia. As far as they were concerned, to be in on the Mafia's action would prove far more lucrative than any of their existing interests. It appears that the Mob were receptive to the idea of forming a business connection with the two London gangsters. Meetings were arranged and business discussed. Satisfied, though still wary, the Americans offered the twins a way of proving themselves. Bonds to the value of $55000 (approximately £336000 in 2018 terms) had been stolen from a Canadian bank. The bonds were far too hot to be moved in North America so, wishing to disperse them as far and wide as possible, the Krays were tasked with selling some of them in Europe. The Mafia watched on closely and the twins were aware that, should they be successful, much more business would come their way.

Just when everything seemed to be going well for Ronnie and Reggie, a dark cloud suddenly appeared on the horizon.

Hew McCowan owned a club in Soho called The Hideaway. The place was well frequented and profitable and as such, could be considered a prime target for extortion. One day McCowan made a complaint to the police. He alleged that the Kray twins were demanding half of the Hideaway's weekly takings. Ronnie and Reggie were quickly arrested and remanded in custody. After spending almost two months awaiting trial, they appeared at the Old Bailey to answer charges of demanding money with menaces. To all on the periphery of the case, it seemed inevitable that the twins would be found guilty and were liable to be given hefty prison sentences. However, in a brilliant counter-stroke, the counsel for the defence informed the court that McCowan was a long-time police informer. Such outlandish claims would often be disregarded because they could not be substantiated. However, on this occasion the barrister had enough documentary proof to throw the reliability of McCowan's evidence into question and as a result the trial was halted and the twins released with no charges to answer.

That very same day, Ronnie and Reggie bought The Hideaway and a lavish welcome home party was thrown to celebrate their release. The Hideaway was to be renamed El Morocco and added to the Krays ever expanding portfolio of west-end ventures....

Five...'Til Death Us Do Part.

By the time of the collapse of the McCowan trial, Reggie Kray had been courting Frances Shea for three years. It is true to say that, for Reggie at least, it had been a case of love at first sight. Here was a local girl who was as beautiful and bubbly as she was innocent to the darker side of life. For her part, Frances wasn't drawn to Reggie because of his power, his money or his reputation; she simply saw in him something that others could not. She had seen Reggie while out and about and knew of his background. Indeed, her brother Frankie was an associate of the Kray gang and would often act as driver for the twins, but that knowledge - knowledge which may have prompted others to run for the hills - did not prevent Frances from eventually succumbing to the attentions of Reggie Kray.

Much to the chagrin of her parents, Frances and Reggie began walking out together. No amount of opposition from her mother and father could persuade young Frances to stop seeing her new beau. Despite all that was said about him, Frances knew Reggie to be a kind and thoughtful man, at least in his dealings with her.

Reggie would often meet her outside her place of work and take her to the cinema. On other occasions there would be drives out into the country and picnics at some remote beauty spot. Other times Reggie would collect Frances from home and take her 'up west', where she would sample the very best that the capitals club scene had to offer. As their relationship blossomed, Reggie proudly showed photos of Frances and himself to anyone within proximity. She was admired for her beauty by all who saw her, and it was often remarked that she bore an uncanny resemblance to the French film star Brigitte Bardot.

After being introduced to Violet and the rest of the Kray clan, Frances became a regular visitor at Vallance Road. Reggie was happy. Business was booming and he had found the love of his life.

For her part, Francis was soon to learn that life with Reggie was not always candlelight and roses. Reggie's time in prison allowed Frances a period to reflect upon their relationship. Although Reggie was keen to marry, it would appear that Frances wasn't so sure. She felt she would never be fully accepted into the Kray family and already had glimpses of what lay in store for her life if she was to consent to becoming Mrs Kray. She was aware that she was already regarded as Reggie's 'property' and knew that he would do his utmost to control her. She had tried to leave him a couple of times, but on each occasion he wooed her back. That Reggie loved her was not up for speculation, but could he prove himself to be the husband Frances wanted?

Despite her reservations, Frances married Reggie in April 1965 at St James' church, Bethnal Green. As to be expected, the church was packed with guests, while outside well-wishers gathered to witness the event. With money no object, the wedding was celebrated with far more than the typical east-end flamboyance. Celebrities were present, and those who couldn't attend sent telegrams expressing their best wishes. In order to capture the day in the best possible way, Reggie engaged the services of the world famous photographer David Bailey.

The newly-weds went off on their honeymoon. Marriage was Reggie's chance to step away from his life of crime. He and Frances could live handsomely on the profits of his legitimate businesses. Could he put his new bride first? Or would she have to play second fiddle to the firm?...

The very thing which had seen the twins rise to the top of the underworld was the same thing which now conspired against them. Yes they had the money, the status and the 'respect', but that could never be enough for the Kray twins. Ronnie in particular was not satisfied. He had but one motive; to prove himself undisputed boss of the London organised crime scene.

Both twins thrived on violence, but for Ronnie it was an almost ethereal experience. He longed for the days of The Regal snooker hall, when he would organise his supporters for raids upon rival outfits in an attempt to slake his unquenchable thirst for savagery. He was constantly looking for new 'threats' which would give him the opportunity to break out the cache of weapons he had stockpiled and mount attacks to shoot, stab, cosh or machete his opponents into submission. Frustratingly, these days, confrontations on this scale always seemed to elude him. His fragile mental health was not helping matters. He took to venting his anger on people who in his eyes had transgressed in some way. To Ronnie, an off the cuff remark or even a wrongly timed glance in his direction were grounds enough to issue a beating, such was his way of thinking. Instances of uncontainable violence involving Ronnie began to soar, his paranoia overtaking him and turning everyone around him into potential enemies.

On one such occasion, an old friend of the twins innocently asked Ronnie if he would lend him £5 (approximately £93 in 2018 terms). Unfortunately the man had mistimed his request, catching Ronnie in the middle of one of his black episodes, and was promptly slashed across the face with a razor sharp blade for his supposed 'affront'.

On a separate occasion, after starting a fight in Esmeralda's Barn, another unfortunate was bundled into a back room where Ronnie branded him across both cheeks with a red hot poker.

Such random acts of mindless violence would never be enough to slake Ronnie's cravings. He wanted someone with whom he and his firm could go to war, just like they did in Capone era Chicago. The problem was, there were no gangs big or brave enough to even contemplate taking the Krays on. Or was there?...

Six...Enter The Richardson's.

In some ways the Richardson brothers were very much like the Krays, yet in others they were polar opposite. Charlie and Eddie shared the twin's enthusiasm for violence, and were both skilled pugilists in their own right. Their reputation preceded them within the shadowy world of London gangland and it was only the foolhardy who chose to get in their way.

Unlike Ronnie and Reggie, the Richardson's had been brought up in a middle-class environment and ran a string of successful legitimate businesses. They were both far more intelligent than the twins and rather than out and out gangsters in the Kray mould, Charlie and Eddie could perhaps better be described as questionable businessmen who saw the use of force as a means to an end rather than the first resort. Put simply, if they could get what they wanted without violence, then they saw no need to employ it. They usually traded on the fact that their reputation alone was often enough to overcome any resistance. That said, they had built up a loyal band of cohorts who were tough and not averse to dishing out punishment to whomever Charlie and

Eddie deemed in need of being taught a lesson.

Whilst a notorious bruiser by the name of George Cornell was in important figure, the Richardson's main henchman was 'Mad' Frankie Fraser. Fraser was a legendary figure throughout the London underworld. Indeed, it is recorded that Mad Frank was the only man Ronnie and Reggie Kray were ever scared of. Physically rather slight in build, Frankie Fraser was nonetheless feared and respected by all those who knew him. The very mention of his name was enough to strike terror into the hearts of many criminals who considered themselves hard men. Despite his slender build, everyone who was anyone knew it was suicidal to cross Frankie Fraser. It would appear that Fraser had a particular loathing for authority and wasn't afraid to slug it out with prison warders during his long periods of incarceration. Fraser had worked for Billy Hill, and was the main culprit in the slashing of Jack Spot. After being released from prison, and despite an approach from Ronnie and Reggie, Fraser was recruited by the Richardson gang where he soon proved himself a vital addition to the team. As one old criminal commented. "The Richardson's getting Frankie Fraser was like China getting the atom bomb!"

While the Richardson's were never known for indiscriminate violence, they were feared for their response to those who sought to do their enterprises harm, or refused to yield to their demands. The gang would often assemble at Charlie's scrap yard in Brixton, where unfortunates would be brought to face their punishment. Such sessions were often conducted in the manner of a mock court, with Charlie even dressing in judges' robes. If a 'defendant' was found guilty then the 'sentence' would be passed and carried out immediately. In this particular department, the Richardson's were often brutally inventive. Aside from the usual beatings, their victims could expect to be tied down then have their teeth pulled out with a pair of old pliers. Some would be whipped, or have cigarettes stubbed out on them. Others would be treated to electric shocks administered from a specially adapted hand cranked military field telephone. Those who were deemed worthy of further punishment were stripped naked and had the terminals of the shock machine attached to their nipples or genitals before being treated to a few turns of the handle. Others were made sit in a bath full of water before being hooked up to the machine.

Another Richardson speciality was the 'Spitmatic'. A tool of the building trade which was used to fire nails into concrete. The gang would use the Spitmatic on the occasions they thought it prudent, and fire it through hands or feet, pinning the victim to the concrete floor. It was actions like these which earned them the nickname 'The Torture Gang'.

Unlike every other criminal outfit in the capital, the Richardson's had no reason to fear the Krays. Why should they? While tensions between the two gangs were always at the simmer, they had co-existed more or less peacefully for some years. However, Charlie and Eddie were confident that if 'the firm' ever ventured south of the river with the intent of muscling in on their action, they would be quickly stopped in their tracks....

The Krays had always carefully monitored the activities of the Richardson gang. That they were heavily engaged in the full gamut of criminal enterprise including protection, fraud, loan sharking, theft and handling stolen goods was known to Ronnie and Reggie. They had long since realised that the profits derived from these activities were worthy of their attention. They acknowledged the Richardson's were a heavy duty outfit, with a lot of talented men behind them, men who wouldn't easily capitulate if ranged against the firm. The fact remained that, as far as Ronnie's own fantasies were concerned, it was unthinkable that the Richardson's should be allowed to operate in a London which was only big enough for one major crime syndicate.

Confrontation was inevitable and Ronnie relished the prospect. He had thought long and hard as to how he intended to deal with the Richardson gang, silently acknowledging that the best route would not only involve what amounted to urban terrorism, but also murder. Ronnie's biggest problem was how he could provide the spark which would ignite the situation and start the war from which the firm would emerge triumphant?

While Reggie continued with his planning, the unofficial cold war between the two gangs came to an abrupt end one evening. While both sides had been expecting and preparing for trouble which they knew would come sooner or later, that night it visited them without warning.

The Astor Club was a well known haunt of the rich and famous. Everyone from royalty to film stars, musicians to international playboys considered the Astor their venue of choice. Given its location, in the heart of wealthy Mayfair, one could be forgiven for thinking that the clubs patrons were drawn exclusively from the ranks of the upper classes and show business celebrities. However, it was also a favourite watering hole of London's most notorious gangsters. Both the Krays and the Richardson's frequented the Astor and one evening they happened to be there at the same time. Tensions between the two groups soon bubbled to the surface and insults were traded. One of the Richardson gang members – a certain George Cornell – rounded off the incident by calling Ronnie "A fat poof."

Somehow, things didn't escalate beyond verbal

abuse and both groups went their separate ways. For the Richardson's and Cornell, the incident was just that, the bumping of heads between men who were not afraid of each other, but for Ronnie Kray it meant war.

To Ronnie's way of thinking, to be called 'a fat poof' by Cornell was unforgivable. He could never allow himself to be demeaned in public in such a fashion, and on this occasion he had a point. If he let one man get away with it, then others would begin to think he was either going soft, or was too afraid to react. Ronnie may have well been a 'poof', but he was neither soft nor scared, and he intended to prove it.

Despite calls for calm from some senior members of the firm, calls which were muted for fear of incurring a beating, it was another incident which cemented Ronnie's hand. Over in Vallance Road, someone who looked like Ronnie had been run over in a hit and run. As far as Ronnie was concerned, this proved that the Richardson's were out to get him. With this 'evidence' in his possession, it didn't take much to persuade Reggie that they should go to war.

Soon after, while the twins were marshalling their forces and finalising their plans, another incident took place at the Astor. The Richardson's main enforcer, the diminutive but highly feared Frankie

Fraser and a few other Richardson associates were entertaining a fugitive Scottish murderer. Kray collaborator Eric Mason and a couple of his friends entered the club. Mason was immediately spotted and insults hurled at him. One of the Richardson's party commented about Mason's friends broken nose, whereupon the man with the broken nose promptly knocked him out. Knifes and hatchets were pulled and a fight ensued. The police were called, and in his rush to escape before they arrived, Mason found himself outside where he was suddenly confronted by Fraser.

"Ronnie and Reggie won't be pleased with what's happened." Mason said. Fraser immediately set about him with an axe before bundling him into a car and driving him to a Richardson owned workshop. Once there Mason was subjected to a sustained and vicious assault with fists and the axe. Barely alive, he was later dumped outside Whitechapel hospital. Mason underwent emergency surgery for three fractures of the skull and a partially severed hand. The other multiple wounds required a total of 370 stitches.

Mason's fate at the hands of Richardson gang members served to give the twins a further sense of urgency. Their preparations continued apace. As soon as they were ready they would strike. Charlie and Eddie, along with their lieutenants would be hit simultaneously. There would be no mercy. The streets of south London would soon be running red with blood.

To Ronnie's consternation, before the offensive could begin the Richardson's found themselves involved in another fight.

The Mr Smith's club in Catford, south-east London, was jointly owned by a Manchester based businessman and an ex-professional wrestler. Despite owning a string of nightclubs in the north-west of England, the two men were unable to effectively handle the clientele of Mr Smiths. They realised they needed help, so turned to old time gangster Billy Hill, who in turn put them in touch with the Richardson's.

The club's owners soon met with Eddie Richardson and Frankie Fraser and a deal was reached whereby the gang would provide door security. As well as protecting the venue, the deal facilitated the installation of Richardson controlled gaming machines. Such machines were becoming widespread through the pubs and clubs of London and accounted for a very healthy income stream for Eddie and Charlie. With the Richardson's now in charge of protecting the club, everyone was confident that the trouble which plagued it would now come to an abrupt end.

The owners of Mr Smith's invited Eddie and Frankie back to the club that evening for a meal and a few drinks. They took up the invitation and duly returned with a couple of other men in tow. During the course of the night they were joined by more and more of the Richardson gang. Eddie, Frankie and their cohorts were determined to enjoy themselves, but had no thought for causing trouble.

Also in the club were a few small time gangsters and a certain Dickie Hart – who was a member of the Kray gang. These men were in a group and watched suspiciously as the Richardson's mob's numbers began to swell. As far as they were concerned, Eddie and Frankie had something planned. Whatever it was it wasn't going to be pretty, and it involved them. One of the group sent out for some weapons in the mistaken belief that they were about to be attacked.

At about 3.30am, Eddie Richardson approached the group and asked them to drink up and leave. It was after closing time and the owners wanted the place cleared. Not knowing that Eddie was acting on behalf of the proprietors, the group took offence and one of them started fighting with Eddie. This was the cue for the other Richardson gang members and a mass brawl broke out. Reports as to what happened next differ but it is understood that Dickie Hart pulled a handgun and began firing indiscriminately around the room, while shouting "Someone's going to die!" In that he was correct, but one wonders if he ever realised it was about to be him.

In the ensuing melee, Hart was shot and fatally

wounded, while Eddie and Frankie Fraser also sustained gunshot wounds. The action had spilled out into the street and, when the sound of police sirens began to break over the scene, everyone split up and made their escape. Fraser didn't get far; he'd been hit in the leg and the wound was severe enough to prevent him from making a getaway. He was found by the police hiding in a nearby garden.

Many of those involved were swiftly rounded up and taken into custody. In one fell swoop, the Richardson gang had been broken up.

Meanwhile, when word of what happened reached the twins, there was much anger. Ronnie took the news badly. He'd been relishing a showdown for some time and had expended much effort preparing his offensive. Now, with almost all the key members of the Richardson gang behind bars, there was no one left to fight.

While most of the Richardson gang had been at Mr Smith's, there were a few who had not attended. Most of the survivors were of no interest to the Kray twins, however, there was one exception. George Cornell was still at large. Ronnie had been quietly raging ever since his encounter with Cornell in the Astor, when he had called Ronnie 'a fat poof'.

For his part, Cornell could not care less about the twins. He wasn't scared of them and would make his feelings known to anyone who listened. It was perhaps this, and his desire to cock a snook at Ronnie and Reggie, which brought him across the river into Whitechapel.

The Blind Beggar pub was only a few streets away from Vallance Road. When someone told Ronnie that George Cornell was drinking there, Ronnie took it as a direct insult. It was also the opportunity he had been waiting for to settle his score with Cornell. Collecting a pistol and taking a couple of men, Ronnie was driven to the pub.

When Ronnie emerged from the Blind Beggar he was elated. He had not only encountered George Cornell but, after squaring off face to face, had shot him in the head. The pleasure Ronnie experienced was almost sexual in its nature. He had committed the ultimate crime and he had committed it in a public place. He had no fear of being caught. No one would dare speak out. He was Ronnie Kray. He was the godfather.

When the police arrived they could get nothing but some scenes of crime photographs. Those who were in the Blind Beggar when the shooting occurred insisted that they hadn't seen anything. Meanwhile, Ronnie and some of the gang went out to celebrate his victory. They were in a pub in Walthamstow when news came that George Cornell was still alive. A contact at the hospital into which

Cornell had been admitted kept Ronnie up to date with events. When the telephone call came through that Cornell had died, Ronnie led his cohorts in a cheer.

Over the coming weeks it became common knowledge that Ronnie Kray was the killer. Although the police heard the same gossip, they were powerless to act. The witnesses still refused to speak up and, apart from Cornell's body, they had no evidence of the crime.

Reggie was acutely aware that the murder of George Cornell would put his brother and him on the police radar. After making sure all evidential links between Ronnie and the shooting were severed – principally by dispatching some of the gang to visit the witnesses and remind them that it would be unwise to talk – he took Ronnie on holiday to Morocco.

Upon their return the twin's realised things had changed. Some of their foot soldiers had distanced themselves from the gang, while the generation of income from illicit means had shrunk after some people stopped paying protection money. The twins were shocked at the rapid deterioration and were quick to reassert themselves and their grip on the city. Those who missed payments soon realised the error of their ways and coughed up all which was owed. There also appeared an air of mistrust within some sections of the firm. If Ronnie could kill

Cornell without real reason, they thought that perhaps they could be next? After all, Ronnie operated on a hair trigger, it would only take a wrong word or even a look to have them joining Cornell.

Seven...Mad Frank.

As far as the twins were concerned, after the Cornell incident and the trouble they experienced when they returned to the UK, they needed a demonstration of their power and influence. After the shooting, it was important to show everyone that they had not slunk off into the shadows, but were out there, as bold as brass and still twice as hard. But what to do?

Frank 'the Mad Axe man' Mitchell was a powerhouse of a man. Such was his strength that he could take a couple of fully grown men by the scruff of the neck and, at arm's length, lift them both at the same time. His other party trick was to single-handedly lift a grand piano. That Mitchell was quite simple-minded was obvious to see; indeed he was sometimes described as having the mind of a child. What he lacked in intellect he more than made up for a propensity for violence. In and out of borstal from an early age, Mitchell soon developed a reputation as a troublesome prisoner. He targeted guards and fellow prisoners alike, his enormous strength making him virtually unstoppable, even when warders were acting in groups. He was eventually classified as 'mentally defective' and sent to Rampton secure hospital. He escaped but, after attacking a member of the public with an iron bar, he was cornered by police. Mitchell didn't allow himself to be recaptured without a fight, attacking the police with two meat cleavers. He was then sent to Broadmoor secure hospital. He escaped again and, after breaking into a private home, held a married couple hostage while armed with an axe. So was born the 'Mad Axe man' alias.

Upon his recapture, Mitchell was given a life sentence and sent to Dartmoor prison. After a while he was allowed out on working parties to conduct labouring tasks on the moors. He proved so difficult to control that, in order to pacify him, the warders often let him wander off on his own. Mitchell would visit local villages and call in at the shops or the pub. This unofficial arrangement suited everyone. Mitchell could have some autonomy while the warders did not face the very real prospect of being attacked and savagely beaten by someone who – although outnumbered – would have little difficulty in defeating them in a physical confrontation.

Ronnie broke the news that he wished to spring Mitchell from prison. At first Reggie was reluctant, but finally relented. Word was got to Mitchell that the Krays would help him escape and from there he could begin a public campaign to petition for his release. Once officially free, the twins knew that, as a fearless and devastatingly effective street fighter, the mighty Mitchell would prove a very useful addition to the firm.

The breakout itself was not a dramatic affair. There was no scaling of walls or sirens wailing. Mitchell simply followed his routine, and after being given the nod by the warders, wandered off on his own from the working party. After making his way to a pre-arranged rendezvous, he was met by a couple of Kray gang members, given a change of clothes, disarmed of the large hunting knife he had made in the prison workshop, then driven to London.

By the time his guards realised that he wasn't coming back from his supposed jaunt to the local pub, it was far too late. It was no less than five hours before the alert was finally raised.

In response to the news of the breakout, the police and military descended upon the moor in force to search for the escaped convict. Roadblocks were set up and the entire area combed. There was a national outcry and questions were asked in parliament when it was revealed that Britain's most violent prisoner could seemingly just come and go as he pleased from outside working parties. As far as many people were concerned, the attitudes of his guards towards Mitchell was not only unforgivable, but unwittingly had actually helped to facilitate his escape. The critics never realised that those charged with overseeing Mitchell during work party detail, were never there in the numbers required to restrain him should he suddenly turn violent. That fact was half a dozen baton wielding prison officers would have proved no match for the axe man.

In the days which followed, and with the help of the Kray gang, Frank Mitchell set about writing to the national press. His complaint was simple. He had behaved himself while in Dartmoor and had been promised by the governor that he would recommend Mitchell be given a release date. Four years after that promise, the release date had never materialised. If the authorities would honour the word of the governor and give him that release date, then he would hand himself in.

Within the midst of the media storm, the then Home Secretary made his own position clear. He refused to negotiate with an escaped felon. He also stated that he would not review Mitchell's case until he was back in custody. This aggrieved Mitchell. In his simplistic way of looking at things, the whole affair was pretty straightforward, yet the authorities didn't want to play his game. He realised that he was caught between a rock and a hard place. To give himself up would mean further jail time and no review, to stay at large meant he would be hunted mercilessly, most likely caught and more time added to his sentence.

As the reality of the situation slowly dawned on him, Mitchell began to get restless. The twins had him holed up in a flat in Barking Road, East Ham, where he was safe from the attentions of the police manhunt. His frustrations grew until he became like a caged tiger. Everyone insisted that he stay indoors. His photo had appeared on the front page of every national newspaper for these past couple of weeks, so chances were he would be recognised before he got halfway down the street. As soon as he was caught, the twins had little reason to doubt that they themselves would be implicated in his escape. However hard they tried, Mitchell wouldn't listen to reason. He wanted to get out and about, to visit his parents and to enjoy himself. As things stood, he concluded that he was more of a prisoner now than he had been while in Dartmoor. He was angry that the twins hadn't been to visit him and made several threats against them. Of course, all this was being reported back to Ronnie and Reggie by the men they had assigned to deal with Mitchell. They also knew that, tough though they were; those men were no match for Frank Mitchell should things suddenly turn physical. In order to calm him down, the twins arranged for a local nightclub hostess to move into the flat. The plan was that she would keep him occupied long enough to allow them to work out a solution to the problem that Mitchell had become.

Though Mitchell was placated somewhat by the arrival of the girl, Ronnie and Reggie decided the only way out of their predicament was to kill him. The firm was mobilised and a plan put together.

On Christmas Eve 1966, Frank Mitchell was collected from the flat. He had been told that he was to be moved to another safe house where Ronnie Kray was waiting to meet him and discuss a new strategy with which he could secure his demands from the Home Office. The plan almost faltered even before it began when Mitchell insisted the girl accompany him. Wary of his brute strength and short temper, the minder who had come to collect him quickly pointed out that it had been arranged she join him the following day. Mitchell wasn't convinced, but calmed down when he was told it was better for security that they travel separately.

Mitchell was led out of the apartment block and into the back of a waiting panel van. Inside the van were several men. As the van accelerated away from the scene these men produced revolvers and opened fire on Mitchell. Approximately twelve shots were put into the big man before he finally succumbed. The minder was dropped off on the corner, whereupon he returned to the flat while Mitchell was removed from the scene.

Mitchell's body was never found, but reports which emerged from those in the know suggests that it was driven down to the coast and put aboard a small boat and, after binding it in chicken wire and weighing it down with rocks, it was dumped in the English Channel.

Eight...Madness, and Heartbreak.

The police investigation into the murder of George Cornell had stalled. They were sure they knew the identity of the killer, but could find no evidence to back up their suspicion.

With Cornell and now Mitchell, the Kray gang members could have been forgiven for thinking that 'the Colonel' (Ronnie) was getting both sloppy and trigger happy. The apparent ease with which he continued to evade the authorities led Ronnie to believe he was invincible. He took to routinely arming himself and had little regard for the possible consequences of brandishing firearms in public places. Indeed, so sure was he that no one would ever testify against him that he actually attempted to shoot someone in the Regency Club. George Dixon was a one time friend of the twins, who had fallen foul of them after making remarks about Ronnie's homosexuality. One evening, in a packed Regency Club, Dixon approached Ronnie to ask why he had been barred. Instead of replying, Ronnie pulled out a pistol, put it to Dixon's head and squeezed the trigger. Instead of a bang there was a click. The gun had misfired! Calmly, Ronnie took the faulty cartridge and handed it to Dixon as a souvenir of their encounter.

Meanwhile, marital bliss had proved short lived for Mr & Mrs Reggie Kray. For reasons known only to himself, Reggie could not and would not allow Frances any semblance of an independent existence. As far as he was concerned, she was his property and he wielded the authority to exercise control over every facet of her life. While he was out attending to business, business which Frances could never understand or be made privy to, she would sit alone in their apartment. On the occasions Reggie did take her out, she would not interact with anyone. The more observant could see that here was an unhappy and confused girl. Arguments were inevitable, and they became increasingly bitter. On one occasion, during a furious row, Reggie deliberately cut his hand and held it over Frances, allowing the blood to trickle onto her. Reggie knew his wife hated the sight of blood, so this made his gesture all the more vile.

Frances was a vivacious, funny, beautiful and intelligent girl, but marriage to Reggie had left her withdrawn and depressed. Aside from Reggie's controlling attitude, she also had Ronnie and Violet to contend with. They made it perfectly clear from the start that she was a Kray in name only and would never be accepted into the family.

Within two months, Frances moved out of the marital home and back in with her parents. Fragile at the best of times, Frances' mental health began to suffer and she was soon receiving treatment for acute depression.

Reggie could not accept that his bride had shunned him. He refused to stay away from Frances, attempting to win her back with promises and gifts. Her medical treatment continued, as did Reggie's constant attention. By this time Frances was well aware of Reggie's criminal activities. Whispers and gossip abounded about the savage exploits of the twins. People distanced themselves from her in the belief that they may somehow find themselves on the receiving end of the Krays wrath. Frances now realised she was as alone here, among her own friend and neighbours, just as much as she had been while living with Reggie. Whilst it seemed to everyone that the pair could not live together, they may also not have been able to live apart.

Frances agreed to reconciliation. That she was as emotionally as brittle as glass and exhausted by events and her ongoing treatment was obvious, yet Frances determined to expose herself to more emotional mistreatment.

Reggie suggested a second honeymoon. She agreed. She was still within the grip of a deep depression, yet appeared a little more upbeat than normal.

Reggie and Francis visited a local travel agent, where they booked a holiday to Ibiza. Time away from London, Ronnie and the firm would do them both good. Frances was staying at her brother's flat and Reggie dropped her there.

A couple of days later, Frances was discovered dead in her bedroom. She had overdosed on barbiturates.

Frances' death demolished Reggie. To those close to him, it seemed that Frances had done what no other person on earth had the power to do – break him. In one final gesture, Reggie gave Frances the funeral to end all east-end send off's. He could do nothing else.

Reggie took to drinking heavily and, as his life unravelled, he became more and more violent. Indeed, it was during this time that he began to match Ronnie in terms of random and senseless brutality.

There were numerous incidents in which Reggie was involved, incidents which – before Frances' death – the victim would probably receive nothing more than a warning or a punch to the head, but now things were different. One incident was sparked when word reached Reggie that a friend of his had disliked Frances. He took two of his cohorts and drove to the man's house. Confronting his victim, Reggie pulled out a pistol and began to shoot. One bullet hit the man in the leg. Before he could do any more damage, Reggie was removed from the scene by his men. The victim was ordered to keep quiet and the incident was not followed up by the police.

Soon afterwards, a second man was shot and wounded in a nightclub when he refused to hand over £1000 (£17100 in 2018 terms) to Reggie. As if to echo his brother, it seemed Reggie had acquired a taste for firearms. Up until now he had only wounded those who found themselves in his sights. How long, the members of the Firm wondered, would it be before they had another Cornell or Mitchell on their hands?

Reggie did not restrict himself to guns, far from it. As many people found to their cost, he would issue punishment beatings or worse for the very slightest of infractions. One unfortunate – an ex professional boxer – was slashed across the face with a knife in the Regency club for doing little more than simply being in the wrong place at the wrong time.

The more senior members of the firm began to get jittery. Reggie, usually the more level headed one of the pair, now seemed to be emulating his brother. All this senseless violence was not good for business, and it exposed the gang to the unwanted attentions of the police. Eventually, and despite the code of silence and fear of retaliation, someone, somewhere, who had become a victim of Ronnie and Reggie's brutality, would present themselves to the police. If they did, then the whole organisation they had all worked so hard to build and preserve would come tumbling down around their ears.

Nine...Jack The Hat.

Despite his personal grief and descent into turmoil, Reggie still had to contend with Ronnie.

Ronnie continued to harbour plans for an expansion of the firm's operations, plans which were largely based upon fantasy. He disliked the fact that Reggie – principally because he was content to stick to what they already had – seemed to be holding his schemes back.

In spite of being a 'fat poof', Ronnie was keen to point out that he was acknowledged as the tougher and more ruthless of the two. As far as he (Ronnie) was concerned, Reggie was soft. After all, he had never even killed anyone. Ronnie goaded his twin at every opportunity, reminding him that he had yet to 'win his spurs'.

Jack 'the hat' McVitie was a notorious east-end criminal and rough houser who had long, if ultimately tenuous, links with the Kray gang. His nickname came about because of his fondness for wearing hats, a habit he had got into in order to disguise his receding hairline. He was an unpredictable character, who liked to inflict pain on others, including women. In one incident, and for no apparent reason than he lost his temper, McVitie threw a woman out of a fast moving car. The lady in question broke her back, but was too scared of possible repercussions to report him to the police.

Recent years had seen the once formidable McVitie overtaken by drink and drugs and it was an unusual set of circumstances which led to the final confrontation between Reggie and Jack.

Ronnie and Reggie, both beset by their own personal problems, had begun to see traitors in their midst. One such person was a man called Leslie Payne. Payne had been a friend of the twins and a partner in various business concerns. In many respects Payne acted as consigliere to the twins, as well as managing the financial aspects of much of their business.

Ronnie and Reggie had reason – most likely unfounded reason – to believe that Payne was about to inform on the activities of the firm to the police. Wishing to distance themselves from what they had planned, they called on Jack McVitie. The proposal was simple. They wanted Payne dead. If McVitie killed him, they would pay him £500 (£8550 in 2018 terms). Desperate for cash to feed his addictions, McVitie accepted the contract. He was given a gun and £100 as an advance payment.

McVitie recruited a friend to help carry out the

job and together they set off for Payne's house. The accomplice was driving the car but began to have second thoughts when McVitie produced a large handgun. For his part, McVitie was worse the wear for drink and most likely drugs, but managed to persuade his friend to see the job through. This unlikely hit team finally made it to Payne's house. Hammering loudly on the door, McVitie was confronted by Payne's wife. He asked to see Payne, but she told him he wasn't in. Seemingly not registering the fact that he was perhaps being lied to, McVitie simply left the scene. That was his one and only attempt on Leslie Payne's life. However, and despite not completing the job, instead of returning the twin's money, he kept it and spent what remained on drink and drugs.

For reasons unknown, and despite protestations from his brother, Reggie seemed keen not pursue the matter of the £100. To Ronnie's disgust, in an effort to smooth matters over, Reggie lent McVitie another £50 (£855 in 2018 terms).

Everyone soon knew that Jack the hat had ripped the twins off for £100. Normally such an infraction would have resulted in swift and merciless retribution. Now, instead of beating McVitie to pulp, here was Reggie giving him more money?! Had the twins started to go soft? If they let Jack McVitie take liberties with their cash, who would be next? Their criminal reputation, a reputation which had been built the hard way over many years, was on the line.

Events took a turn for the worse when a drunken McVitie turned up the Regency club. He had armed himself with a sawn-off shotgun and was ranting and raving that he was going to shoot the twins.

Word of Jack the hat's latest escapade soon found its way back to Vallance Road. As soon as it reached the ears of Ronnie and Reggie, McVitie's fate was sealed.

Orders were issued. McVitie was to be found. Despite the best efforts of the firm, somehow McVitie evaded the dragnet, but soon enough the twins heard that he was planning to visit the Regency on the night of 28th October 1967. On that same night, the twins were throwing a party for their mother and family friends at a local pub. Armed with a small .32 pistol, Reggie slipped away from the party and was driven to the Regency where he lay in wait for McVitie.

McVitie failed to show. Angry and frustrated, Reggie left the pistol with the club's manager and made his way to another party at a flat in Cazenove Road.

Ronnie was already in attendance at the flat and keen to hear the details of his brother's encounter with Jack the hat. When he learned that Reggie had 'failed him' once again, Ronnie resolved that immediate action was required to put an end to the McVitie situation once and for all.

He sent one of his cousins to retrieve the gun from the Regency and ordered two of his most trusted Lieutenants to find McVitie and bring him to Cazenove Road. Ronnie then set about laying the trap. He cleared the flat of all the party-goers and warned them all they were not to speak about the evening or having seen the twins. Soon, the only people left were Ronnie, Reggie and a few of their senior cohorts.

The two men Ronnie sent looking for McVitie had tracked their prey down and persuaded him to join them at an all night party. They assured McVitie that there was plenty of birds and booze to be had. McVitie readily accepted the invitation.

Meanwhile, the gun which Reggie left at the Regency had turned up at the flat. The ambush was now missing but one vital component.

Shortly before midnight the two firm members returned. With them was Jack McVitie. Drunk, McVitie burst into the room.

"Where's the birds and the booze?!" He announced.

There were no women and no alcohol, instead the Kray twins and a few others were waiting to receive him. Stepping out from behind the door through which McVitie had just entered, Reggie had the gun to the back of his head. McVitie froze, the sudden realisation of the situation instantly sobering him. Without further ado, Reggie pulled the trigger.

Misfire! Reggie grabbed at McVitie, but Jack the Hat managed to struggle free. In the milliseconds which followed, Jack realised there was only one avenue of escape open to him. Launching himself forwards, he attempted to throw himself through the window. He almost managed to escape, but was caught by the legs and dragged back inside the room.

"Be a man, Jack!" Ronnie said, as he took hold of McVitie's arms and pinned them behind his back.

"I'll be a man." McVitie replied, tears now rolling down his cheeks. "But I don't want to fucking die like one."

While this was happening, Reggie had picked up a carving knife and drove it into McVitie's face, just below the eye socket. With Ronnie still holding the wildly struggling McVitie, Reggie plunged the knife repeatedly into his chest and stomach until McVitie was dead.

Shortly afterwards the twins left the scene. They had ordered that McVitie's body be disposed of and the scene of the crime cleared of any trace of the murder.

Various rumours still abound as to the fate of Jack the Hat's corpse. Theories subscribed to include that it was buried beneath a tower block which was being constructed at the time, that it was burned in the furnaces of a power station, or that it was chopped up and fed to pigs. Whatever its end, the body has never been recovered.

The gun and the knife were dropped into the Thames while the only other piece of hard evidence – the flat – was given a thorough going over by members of the firm. Blood was swabbed from the floors and walls and the whole place was redecorated and had new carpets fitted. Nobody, not even those present on that fateful night, could tell that a murder had taken place there.

Secure in the knowledge that no witnesses would ever come forward, or reports of a murder reach the police, the twins went back to their day to day duties. After all, they had got away with the killings of George Cornell and Frank Mitchell, and there were no indicators to suggest they wouldn't do the same with Jack McVitie.

Ten...Closing The Net.

The Kray's stranglehold on gangland London remained as tight as ever. If anyone interpreted recent history as a sign that the Kray's star was beginning to wane, then they were quickly proved wrong. The fate of Cornell, Mitchell and latterly Jack the Hat, soon dispelled any notion that the firm had lost its grip. Things continued as normal – or as normal as they could ever be for Ronnie and Reggie. They were cold-blooded murderers and no one could touch them or interfere with the workings of their criminal empire. As with their first two victims, the story surrounding Jack McVitie's death was an open secret, but the twins were confident in thinking that nobody would ever be foolish enough to inform on them.

During these past months, news of events (mainly delivered by anonymous letter) had been filtering in to Scotland Yard. The police had plenty of reason to place Ronnie and Reggie at the top of their list of suspects for the triple murders, and ample cause to link them to countless acts of violence and racketeering. However, every shred of 'evidence' they possessed was purely circumstantial. Hearsay was no good in court, so if the police were to successfully prosecute the twins and bring down the firm, it was vital that they had a watertight case based upon witness statements from people whom a court would consider as credible.

The fact remained that nobody would come forward to give testimony of the Krays involvement in murder and organised crime.

That the Metropolitan Police kept an open file on the Krays was known to the firm. If nothing else, their willingness to openly associate themselves with celebrity assured that the Met would wish to keep tabs on them. Police activity surrounding the twins variously consisted of intelligence gathering via informants, or occasional observation, but little more. Sometimes, when the police were showing a particular interest, plain clothed officers would park up on Vallance Road in an unmarked car to watch the comings and goings at the Kray's family home. More often than not, Reggie or Ronnie would take a tray of tea and biscuits out to them as reminder that they knew why they were there.

For a long time there seemed no prospect of gathering the hard evidence required to arrest, let alone charge, Ronnie or Reggie. The east-end wall of silence was proving as impenetrable as ever.

It was a whole six months after his murder that the police became aware of the disappearance of Jack McVitie. Rumour abounded, but it was just that – rumour. It appeared that the cycle of dead end leads and absolute non co-operation would play itself out once more in any investigation into Jack McVitie's suspected slaying, causing any case the police attempted to build to grind to a fruitless halt.

After reviewing this most unsatisfactory of situations, Scotland Yard's most senior officers were unanimous in their agreement that if they were to finally bring the Krays and their firm to justice, they would need a whole new strategy.

Leonard Ernest Read was a diminutive figure, his lack of stature earning him the nickname 'Nipper'. Born in Nottingham, he had served with the Royal Navy during WW2, where he achieved the rank of Petty Officer. He was a successful amateur boxer and one time lightweight champion. Read joined the Met in 1947, just scraping in at the minimum height requirement of 5'7". Read soon established a reputation as a talented officer. After specialising as a detective with the CID (Criminal Investigation Department), Read began to rise through the ranks. He participated in the investigation of many high profile cases, including the great train robbery. By the time he was approached to undertake a new job he was a Detective Chief Superintendent and a member of the Met's famous Murder Squad.

After being summoned to attend a meeting, the detail of which he was not made privy to beforehand, Read's bosses at Scotland Yard gave him a comprehensive briefing on the situation regarding the Kray twins as it pertained to them.

They knew that, as long as the Krays and their gang remained hidden behind the wall of silence, they could never be evidentially tied to past or even future murders, acts of violence or criminal enterprise. It seemed that the police would continue to be powerless to intervene.

Read's tasking was both simple yet highly complicated. He would assemble a small handpicked team of the Met's best detectives – officers whose professional integrity was beyond question – and lead them in an operation to bring down the Krays.

It was long suspected (and true) that the twin's influence had reached into parts of the police service. Corrupt officers quick to make a quick buck would tip them off about police activity which may affect them and their illegal activities. In order to lessen the chances of the firm being made aware of this new initiative, it was decided that Read's new unit would not use Scotland Yard as its base; instead it would operate from a place which had no connection to the Met.

Tintagel House was a block of government buildings located on the south bank of the river Thames. This unofficial task force headquarters was isolated from the rest of the police service and all but essential contact could be severed. The cover story for this new team – to keep their activities a secret from those who may otherwise inform on them to the twins – was that they were investigating a murder which had occurred in Northern Ireland.

As soon as they settled in to their new HQ, Read's new team set about their undertaking with quiet efficiency. They had been warned from the start not to speak about anything they were doing or planning to do to anyone outside the team, as the success of their mission hinged upon complete secrecy.

It was only when they began to dig deeper that they became truly aware of the enormity of the task which lay before them. They were working clandestinely, and very much on the sidelines. From Tintagel House, they hoped to gather evidence against the twins where everyone else had failed.

Reaching out cautiously to underworld figures and others who may prove useful in building the case against the twins soon proved fruitless. No one wanted to talk. It mattered not if they held grudges against the Krays, or that they had been beaten, stabbed or shot. They would not break their silence. Despite their efforts, at one point it was feared that the new task force's investigation would go the way of all other attempts to corner the twins – that was until Nipper Read received an unexpected break.

Eleven...Breaking The Silence.

Leslie 'The Brain' Payne was a long standing associate of Ronnie and Reggie. As already mentioned, he acted as fixer, front man, financial advisor for the twins, and had overseen many of their business dealings. Payne wasn't the typical gangster type; indeed, he bore no resemblance to any of the firm's other members. This most unlikely of accomplices looked and acted every inch the city businessman. He lived quietly with his wife and two daughters in a respectable area of town. He did not openly associate himself with the twins on the club circuit, nor did he court publicity. He was the typical 'grey man', contenting himself with going about his business without creating the same bow waves which seemed to continually accompany Ronnie and Reggie.

Payne's association with the firm had been highly profitable for all involved. His acumen bringing in substantial amounts of money from business interests which otherwise would not have been open to the twins. The combination of Ronnie and Reggie's muscle and Payne's subtle entrepreneurial skills had proved a winning formula alright, but one which ultimately was to turn sour.

In recent times, the twins had become convinced that Leslie Payne was double crossing them in business and also secretly speaking to the police. They were incorrect on both counts, and had no evidence with which to back up their suspicions. However, and unlike the police, Ronnie and Reggie had little need for evidence, mere suspicion of double dealing being enough to warrant punishment for the supposed perpetrator.

Despite their best efforts to give him the impression that all was well, Payne was aware that the twins regarded him as a liability. He was also aware that they had recently ordered a hit on him. Ironically, the would be assassin had been none other than Jack McVitie.

Although no more attempts had been made upon his life, Payne was conscious of the fact that, as far as the twins were concerned, the 'problem' continued to fester. Could he – Payne – smooth things over with Ronnie and Reggie and return their relationship back onto an even keel? He doubted it. Although they seemed to have gone off the idea of murdering him, nothing he could say would be enough to fully satisfy the twins of his loyalty to them and the firm. Even if they believed him, Payne knew it wouldn't take much to land him back in the twin's sights. As far as he was concerned, at some point Ronnie and Reggie had the same fate as McVitie, Cornell and Mitchell in store for him.

With the sword of Damocles hanging above his head, Payne the brain began to weigh up his options. He knew they were extremely limited, and the only one with any chance of success was itself fraught with dangers, not only for Payne, but for his family too.

Leslie Payne made contact with the police and soon found himself removed from circulation and ensconced in a hotel room in Marylebone. Knowing that his wife and children were receiving police protection, he could relax a little. The Met were also taking no chances when it came to making sure no harm came to this potential star witness. During his stay, armed officers in plain clothes were present in the neighbouring rooms and Payne himself was never without the company of at least one armed bodyguard. For use when he returned home, he was also given a telephone number with which he could have direct access to Read's team at any time of the day and night.

When Payne met Nipper Read he didn't know quite what to make of him. He had heard about the Chief Superintendent and knew of his reputation as a gifted detective. For his part, Read was at pains to put his new informant at ease and soon the two men became relaxed in each other's company.

The next three weeks was spent carefully extracting information from Leslie Payne. The statement Payne finally put his signature to was the most comprehensive account of the firm's activities the police had ever seen. It ran to an astounding two hundred pages long and detailed everything from their illicit business dealings throughout London, to their connection with the American Mafia.

Keeping his bosses at Scotland Yard informed of the progress of the investigation, everyone was keenly aware that – despite the explosive nature of Payne's testimony – they now needed to verify all his claims. The nature of the investigation meant that they could not arrest the Krays and the other members of the firm on the evidence of just one man. If they went down this route, all their hard work would go to waste. If it ever reached court, everyone concerned knew that the defence would destroy Payne and render his witness statement useless. For it to be of real evidential value, everything Payne had told them would have to be substantiated by others.

Nipper Read's team began to backtrack through the list of people they had already interviewed. Those people, who had all refused to speak out first time round, were now given an assurance that any statements they made would not be used until after the twins, and indeed the rest of the firm, had been arrested and held in custody.

Despite the secrecy surrounding the police operation, it was perhaps inevitable that word of

Nipper Read's mission to bring them to justice would filter back to the twins. Although they were now aware that the Met had a special squad dedicated to investigating the activities of the firm, Ronnie and Reggie were not in possession of any real detail surrounding Read's efforts. They certainly didn't know about Payne or his statement, or that Read's team were quietly busying themselves eliciting more evidence from others.

As a joke, and to send a message to the Met, the twins bought themselves a couple of pet python snakes and named them after the two detectives who irked them the most. One of the snakes was called 'Nipper'. Unfortunately for Ronnie and Reggie, just like his namesake, Nipper proved too hard to handle. Perhaps, just perhaps, their little joke was a foretaste of events to come?

While the Kray twins continued to cock a snook at the police, Nipper Read and his team carried on with their operation. Ronnie especially was obviously unconcerned about the Met's interest. As far as he was concerned the police had nothing but second hand accounts about the murders and wider illegal activities the firm. Nothing, absolutely nothing, in the Met's possession could be used as evidence against them in a court of law.

It was during this time, a time when they should have reigned themselves in until the heat was off, that Ronnie decided he wanted to extend his contact with the Mafia.

Despite the fact that Ronnie's criminal record forbade him from entering the United States, a contact in the US embassy was approached by a new business associate of the twins and a visa duly issued.

Ronnie and the business associate – a one Alan Cooper – soon found themselves aboard a New York bound aeroplane. Once in the city, a series of meetings took place between Ronnie, Cooper, and a representative of the Mafia.

After their return to London, and via Cooper, Ronnie became aware that the Mafia would appreciate the firm's help. The Mob wanted someone dead and they were looking to the twins to carry out the hit. As far as Ronnie was concerned, this new assignment only added fuel to his fantasies of becoming the undisputed godfather of London's gangland. If the firm proved themselves worthy and capable of carrying out Mafia wishes, then the possibilities for business – and the potential for limitless financial gain – was virtually assured.

Alan Cooper was proving himself a valuable asset as the twin's new business advisor. He seemed to have unfettered access to people and things which would normally be out of bounds to even the twins. As a result he had quickly displaced Leslie Payne as consigliere to the firm. Ronnie in particular was very impressed with Cooper's performance and soon found himself trusting the man beyond what someone his position should. However, in Ronnie and Reggie's eyes, during their short association, Cooper had proved himself as absolutely trustworthy. After all, he had already helped the twins to dispose of stolen bonds, now it seemed he was both eager and willing to assist in this new caper.

The man the Mafia wanted dead was a London based Maltese club owner. There was no reason given as to why the hit had been ordered and no questions asked, the firm simply began to plan his demise.

While most others warned that the best way to approach the problem was to just make the target disappear, or wait until the police investigation against them had run out of steam, Ronnie wanted something suitably dramatic. If he was to impress his colleagues across the Atlantic, then the hit would be best performed Chicago gangster style.

It would be a risky, even foolish, move yet Ronnie insisted that to make a statement which would make the Mafia sit up and take notice would require far more than simply causing the target to vanish or be found floating down the Thames with a bullet in his head. No, that would never do.

While in conference with Cooper, Ronnie announced that he planned to kill the club owner by placing a bomb under his car. This act of terrorism on the streets of London would be sure to bring the full weight of the police and perhaps even the domestic security service, MI5, down upon the firm, but Ronnie was adamant. His way was the best way of achieving the strategic aims of the firm and finally cementing their relationship with the American syndicate.

To everyone in the firm's surprise, Cooper seemed enthusiastic about Ronnie's plan. He informed Ronnie that he had a contact in Scotland who could supply explosives. Without further ado, and upon Ronnie's order, Cooper dispatched an assistant of his to collect four sticks of dynamite. The man arrived in Glasgow, made contact with Cooper's associate, and took possession of the explosives.

Although they were ignorant of the plot to kill the club owner, Nipper Read's team were maintaining a close watch on the movements of both the twins and the firm's senior members. Possibly as a result of telephone tapping, Read was aware of the reason why Cooper's man had travelled to Scotland. As he made to board the flight home, the man was arrested. Caught bang to rights in possession of dynamite and facing serious charges, including conspiracy to commit murder, the man quickly named Cooper as the person who had ordered the collection of the explosives.

Knowing they had little time to waste, Nipper

Read's team brought Cooper in for questioning. Nipper was shocked to learn that, rather than being the shady 'fixer' that both he and the twins (indeed even the Mafia) thought him to be, Cooper was actually an agent of the US Treasury Department.

After making contact with the federal authorities to corroborate what Cooper had told them, it transpired that the Americans were themselves investigating the links between their own organised crime groups and the Kray twins, and had a particular interest in the fate of stolen bonds. Read was also made aware that Cooper had been operating covertly with the full knowledge of Scotland Yard's top brass. Wary that perhaps even Read's handpicked team may contain an informer, they had agreed to Cooper's mission and kept it on a purely need to know basis.

Being an outsider, Cooper and his own team of men had no possible connection with the Krays beyond that which they had forged themselves. It stood to reason that their operation could not be compromised in the way that so many of the previous Met's attempts had been.

Read was aghast, it would appear that even he wasn't trusted?! As it related to the British police, and in return for co-operation in the US Treasury Department investigation, Cooper's mission had been to incriminate the twins in the attempted murder of the club owner by having them arrested while they were in possession of the dynamite.

Everyone knew that this mission was now dead in the water. News of the couriers arrest and Cooper's own detention would now be in the hands of the firm. The only way forward which Nipper read could see was to use Cooper himself as bait to entrap the twins.

'Suffering' from a bogus medical complaint, Cooper was released into hospital. Hoping that news would leak from the decidedly un-watertight Scotland Yard, Read let it be known that he didn't have enough evidence to charge Cooper in connection with the dynamite, thus had been forced to release him pending further inquiries.

Before his admission to hospital, Read briefed Cooper on the forthcoming sting. The private room which Cooper was to occupy had been wired for sound by Met technicians with the result that all subsequent conversations which took place therein could be recorded. Cooper was instructed to invite the twins to the hospital, where he would speak to them about the failure of the dynamite plot. It was hoped that Ronnie and Reggie would talk their way into enough trouble to allow themselves to be arrested and charged with conspiracy to commit murder. This charge – although serious – was not on the same scale as murder, however Read hoped that by removing the twins and some of their senior Lieutenants from the scene, would embolden those who were still proving reluctant to talk to finally make statements.

Cooper made a telephone call to the twins from his hospital bed. He invited them to visit and discuss 'unfinished business'. Something – perhaps a sixth sense – alerted Ronnie and Reggie to the fact that all was not as it should be. They were unsettled by Cooper's manner and this unusual request. Cooper should have known better than to want to speak about 'hot' topics in an environment which was not under the control of the twins? Indeed, they were so suspicious that they sent a representative in their place. The man, a trusted associate, was ordered not to speak about anything relating to the proposed murder, or any other of the firm's business matters. Should Cooper attempt to lead him, he was to feign innocence and only reply that he, Ronnie or Reggie, had no idea what he was talking about.

After leaving the hospital the man was to immediately report back to the twins and give his account of the meeting along with any suspicions he may have about Cooper.

Afterwards, when their man returned from the hospital visit, cross-examining led the twins to conclude that their misgivings had indeed been justified. They didn't know his game, but they now knew they could not trust Alan Cooper. The police – and principally Nipper Read – must have got to Cooper? Had the police offered him a way out of his predicament with the dynamite by getting him to incriminate Ronnie and Reggie?

For his own personal safety, Cooper was immediately recalled to the USA and the operation he had headed up put on ice.

From Nipper Read's perspective, the meeting was a disaster. Although Cooper had attempted to reel his visitor in with leading questions, the man did not bite. All the recordings contained were Cooper's own voice and the decidedly non-incriminating answers of his visitor. As far as any third party was concerned, the man had simply confirmed that Ronnie and Reggie had no idea what Cooper was speaking about, let alone being complicit in an attempted murder.

Read's exasperation at how events had spiralled beyond his control was justifiable. All the months of quiet detective work by his dedicated team of officers had seemingly gone for naught. In their desperation to ensnare the Kray twins, his bosses at Scotland Yard had become complicit in another operation, an operation involving a foreign law enforcement agency. They had not deemed it relevant to inform Read so, perhaps inevitably, the US Treasury Department mission and that of his own squad had collided. From the wreckage, the only ones to emerge unscathed were Ronnie and Reggie.

With security surrounding his operation now compromised and the twins expecting further attempts upon their liberty, it seemed to everyone that the Met was right back where they had started. Had all the efforts of Read's special investigation team been for nothing?

Twelve...Catch Us If You Can.

For the twins, but especially Ronnie, this latest brush with the law had reinforced their sense of invincibility. However hard the police tried, they simply could not build a case against the firm. That said, Ronnie and Reggie now had a measure of just how much time and effort the police were expending on investigating the activities of the firm, Cooper's actions alone confirming that those same police actions were far more serious than the twins had first imagined. It was a warning shot which they could not afford to ignore.

Despite the feeling of triumphalism at defeating whatever plot in which Cooper had become embroiled, it was quickly agreed by all involved that the firm must tread lightly in the coming months and years. This didn't signal an end to their numerous criminal activities, but a seismic shift in the way those same activities were approached was required. Even Ronnie agreed that if the firm was to remain one step ahead of the police, then they would have to withdraw into the shadows. Until they were completely satisfied that the heat was off, gone was the mindless and often random acts of violence, supplanted instead by a more businesslike approach to the running of the Kray empire.

That the twins had chosen this path was yet another source of frustration for the authorities. However, and contrary to popular belief at the time, things weren't all going the way Ronnie and Reggie wanted.

Although business remained good, and profits from their numerous concerns kept flowing in, it would appear that life had lost a little of its lustre for the twins. They became increasingly frustrated at how their own personal desire for violence was being curtailed. This wasn't the way the infamous Kray twins operated. Their whole existence within the criminal underworld had been founded their reputation as fearless hard men. The new approach to their dealings meant that, for the first time, their skills as fighters were redundant. They were now forced to trade on reputation rather than action. Those surrounding them, allies and enemies alike, were under no illusion that this new chapter in the firm's history did not signal that Ronnie and Reggie had gone soft. It meant that – perhaps – the police had made more of an impact upon the firm than was first thought possible.

It had been almost six months since the abortive attempt to entrap the twins by Cooper. Although they were aware that Scotland Yard continued to monitor their activities, both Ronnie and Reggie remained confident that the police had nothing but circumstantial evidence with which to link them to their crimes.

The new low key strategy of conducting the firm's business affairs was also proving successful. Neither the twins nor any of their close associates had stuck their heads above the parapet in all this time, giving the police no opportunity to arrest, let alone charge. People on both sides of the fence with interests in the case were resolving themselves to the fact that Ronnie and Reggie had once again beaten the system. The mood in Scotland Yard was black. If the firm continued to operate in this manner, and if no new evidence was forthcoming, then the Kray twins would truly place themselves beyond the reach of the law once and for all.

Financed by the money from their illicit enterprises, the twins and the rest of the firm were enjoying the good life. Everyone was now buoyed by their belief that that they could escape the attentions of the Met. The only fly in the ointment was the fact that the firm's new direction continued to go completely against the grain. Ronnie, Reggie and many of the firm's senior members thrived on violence and mayhem. Even if the police could not directly intervene to stop the activities of the gang, the fact that they knew they were being watched slowly began to take its toll on all concerned.

In order to lift the mood, one day Ronnie decided on a 'works outing'. He instructed his cohorts to bring along their women and join Reggie and him at the Astor Club for an evening of drinking and entertainment.

The photographers who always gathered outside the Astor to snap its celebrity clientele were more than happy to expend a few rolls of film on the twins and their guests as they arrived at the club. Unusually, and adhering to the firm's new under the radar approach, Ronnie was not pleased by the attention of the press pack. Still, aside from a few comments, he made little fuss and entered the building in the company of the young man he had invited along as his guest.

As predicted, a good night was had by all. It wasn't until 5am the following morning that the twins left the club to make their way back to their flat in Finsbury.

No sooner than the twins retired to bed to sleep off the excesses of the night that the door to their apartment was suddenly smashed off its hinges. The police were armed and there in force and leading them was Nipper Read. Before Ronnie and Reggie could react, they were arrested and handcuffed. Nipper Read himself made the arrest and closely oversaw the removal of the twins from the apartment block to the waiting convoy of police vehicles.

While the raid on the twin's flat was taking place, more teams of armed police struck at the addresses of the rest of the gang. A couple of the firm's members managed to slip the net because they weren't at home, however they too were quickly rounded up in the following days.

Nipper Read was in the process of undertaking the greatest gamble of his police career, a gamble which – if it went wrong – would cost him not only his professional reputation but in all likelihood his job. With Ronnie, Reggie and the rest of the firm's leading members in custody, he would invoke the clause contained within the statements of the few witnesses he had persuaded to testify against them.

Read's whole case against Ronnie and Reggie was built on sand, and he knew it. What little witness evidence he and his team had gathered against the firm was barely enough to secure any convictions. This weakness was noted with grave concern within the corridors of power at Scotland Yard. Everyone dealing with the case was aware that, in addition to the frailty of their position, they had absolutely no evidence whatsoever to link either of the twins to the killing of Cornell, Mitchell and McVitie. As things stood, if the case against the twins and the firm went to court, there was every chance it would be thrown out. Each charge made against them would have to be proven beyond reasonable doubt. Given nature of the crimes and the backgrounds of the people who would testify, the defence would have ample room for manoeuvre in their attempts to return not guilty verdicts. Read, his colleagues and commanders knew that should the case collapse, then it would mark the end of all police operations against Ronnie and Reggie.

The only ace Read held was his ability to approach those people who were still reluctant to speak to him. If he could assure them that they would not be in danger should they provide statements, then the case against the Kray twins could be strengthened to the point where it could be put before the court with reasonable chance of success.

As far as Ronnie and Reggie were concerned there was no need for panic. They remained confident that they and their legal representatives were on top of the police case. From their cells in Brixton prison, they made sure word went out to their associates who were incarcerated alongside them, as well as those who remained free, that the Kray twins considered this latest police action as merely a blip, a throw of the dice by a desperate enemy. Once their lawyers had worked their magic, everyone would be released and then it would be business as usual.

With a few of the firm still at large, Nipper Read knew that those who had most to offer in terms of providing crucial evidence were the ones who were most fearful of retribution. Read's squad moved quickly to round up the Krays outer circle, the ones whom Nipper thought most likely to carry out the twins orders to intimidate any potential witness.

With the last vestiges of the firm cleared from the streets, the police could now concentrate its efforts upon securing those all important statements.

Brick by brick, the wall of silence that had surrounded and protected the twins for so long was slowly demolished. People began to emerge from the shadows to provide written affidavits. The testimony was wide ranging and eventually proved strong enough to turn the tide. Now Nipper Read found himself with more than a fighting chance of securing guilty verdicts against not only the twins, but many of their senior Lieutenants.

For the very first time, after initial hearings at the Old Bailey, cracks began to emerge within the firm itself. One of the twin's former associates – a man who had assisted with the escape of Frank Mitchell and had helped in the cleanup operation after the Murder of Jack McVitie – took to the witness box to deliver a statement. Despite the withering stares of the twins and other members of the firm, the witness gave over his evidence. To the firm's surprise, he was followed by the barmaid who was on duty in the Blind Beggar on the night of George

Cornell's death. She told the court what she had seen that fateful night, before going into detail about how she was then warned to keep quiet by men who had identified as representatives of Ronnie and Reggie.

The woman's statement was damning and came as a shock to everyone present. Ronnie, Reggie and the other accused were dumbstruck by her submission to the court. First they'd seen their friend take the stand to give a statement against and now this?! It the police had managed to persuade these people to come in on the side of the prosecution, then who else would be sprung upon them at trial?

At the end of the preliminary hearings, the twins and their associates were ordered to remain on remand until commencement of the trial.

Finally, in acknowledgement that things were now going seriously awry, Ronnie and Reggie set about a programme of damage limitation. As far as they were concerned there was still no hard evidence with which to link them to the murders. If anyone was to be charged and convicted of the killings of Cornell, Mitchell and McVitie, then both twins were determined to make sure it wouldn't be them. Getting word out through runners, they set out their plan to the other members of the firm. While they – Ronnie and Reggie – would take some of the lesser charges, they expected their cohorts to shoulder the blame for the more serious offences, including the murders. The twins attempted to assure their men that they and their families would be well looked after while they were in prison. It soon became clear that saying no to this scheme was not an option.

To be sentenced for crimes they had committed was one thing, but to take the blame for something they had no part of was another. If those involved in this last escapade went along with it, they knew that Ronnie and Reggie could expect no more than ten years apiece. If they behaved themselves they could expect to be released in as little as half that time. For someone sentenced to murder, it would be another matter entirely. Life sentences would be given and these would have to be served concurrently with others should they be found guilty of racketeering and associated crimes.

Nipper read, aware of the twins plotting, visited each member of the firm individually with the aim of getting them to talk. Of course, they would never incriminate themselves, but with luck and a following wind, they may just be persuaded to provide evidence against Ronnie and Reggie.

Conceding that there was no way out of the predicament, and not wishing to commit themselves to decades in prison for crimes they did not commit, a few of the firm began to open up.

Soon Read and his team had amassed statements

which together told a story of the full scale of the twin's crimes. Included within these testimonies were graphic accounts of the murders of Cornell, and McVitie.

Thirteen...Nemesis.

The trial of the Kray twins commenced on the 7th of January 1969. When it started the police had accrued more than enough testimony to have the twins charged with murder.

From the off, Ronnie and Reggie knew they were facing an uphill struggle. By now many of their most trusted companions had deserted them, crossing the bench to turn Queen's evidence. As the trial continued, it became obvious to Ronnie and Reggie that they had no chance of escaping guilty verdicts.

In the end, some twenty-eight men gave evidence against the Kray Twins. Their underworld activities and acts of murder – which for so long had only been spoken of in muted whispers – were finally brought to the attention of the world. The courtroom was packed to capacity during every session, with tickets to the public gallery on sale by touts at £5 each (£75 in 2018 terms).

Such was the twins list of contacts and national interest in the case, that many celebrities turned up to watch the proceedings, while other who were unable to attend sent messages of support to Ronnie and Reggie.

Many people, famous or no, were there out of curiosity, but others were fearful that they too may be named or somehow implicated – by mere association – with the firm's crimes. No doubt, senior establishment figures were also wary of what Ronnie and Reggie might have to say. Whoever these people were, and whatever secrets they wished to protect, they had no reason to fear. While the twins were white hot with rage at the duplicitous behaviour of their former friends and colleagues, they were equally determined not to stoop to the levels which they were now witnessing. The twins were many things, but they weren't 'grasses'. They would never speak to the police, or offer witness statements in order to lessen their punishment, that was their criminal 'code of honour'; though that same code didn't appear to extend to attempting to wriggle free by getting their friends to take the blame for many of their more serious crimes.

When the time came for the twin's themselves to take to the stand, those spectating were not disappointed. Despite the overwhelming weight of evidence which had been brought to bear against them, Ronnie and Reggie refused to yield. Whilst under cross examination, Ronnie maintained the notion that he had killed George Cornell was ludicrous. Cornell, Ronnie maintained, was a boyhood friend of theirs (which was true). Despite what the witnesses said, he had never visited the Blind Beggar on the night in question.

Reggie was equally adamant that he had nothing to do with the death of Jack McVitie. What of all the testaments to the contrary? They had been made as a result of police malpractice, by people looking to save their own skins, or had come from the mouths of those who held grudges. For those very same reasons, nothing the prosecution had offered as evidence, they argued, should be taken seriously by the court. In actual fact they were making pertinent point, points which the jury would have to consider very carefully. Were Ronnie and Reggie the victims of people who, for whatever reason, were out to get them?

The twins retained their composure throughout the trial, save for a couple of occasions. Ronnie called the prosecuting counsel 'a fat slob' when it was announced to the court that the police had confiscated his grandparent's pension books. Reggie screamed that 'the police are scum' while details of his late wife's death was being read to the court.

The outcome of the trial was inevitable. After sixty one electrifying days, the verdict of the jury was delivered. The presiding Judge, Justice Melford Stevenson, a notoriously harsh man with a reputation for handing out maximum sentences, saw no need to exempt the firm from his ways. Those few cohorts who had refused to assist the police and remained loyal to Ronnie and Reggie were each handed stiff sentences ranging from ten to twenty years. Among the guilty was Charlie Kray – Ronnie and Reggie's older brother – who received ten years for helping to dispose of Jack McVitie's body.

In his closing speech, Justice Melford Stevenson remarked to Ronnie and Reggie. "I am not going to waste words on you. In my view society has earned a rest from your activities. I sentence you to life imprisonment, which I recommend should not be less than thirty years."

The pronouncement drew gasps from those attending the court. Thirty years minimum?! Ronnie and Reggie were thirty-four years old. By the time they were eligible for release, they would only be a year short of state pension age.

If the thought that they would have to spend at least three decades in prison wasn't enough, the twins knew that the authorities had not yet finished with them. There was the matter of Frank Mitchell. Also, many of their other criminal operations still had to be answered for.

They were eventually tried for the murder of the mad axe man. While they admitted to harbouring him after his escape, there was insufficient evidence to convict them of his murder. The processes of law surrounding other potential charges ground on slowly, but eventually came to a halt but the file on the Kray twins many other criminal activities was left open.

After all the dust settled, all that remained was for Ronnie and Reggie and their small band of loyal followers to accept their fate and adapt themselves to prison life.

Thirteen...Epilogue.

Ronnie and Reggie Kray never did make parole. Throughout their sentence, the authorities were adamant that they should not be allowed to return to society. The pair wiled away their time writing accounts of their crimes, dreaming of freedom and even painting pictures.

If one thing prison did for the Krays, then it was to elevate their status among people who were too young to remember or really appreciate the gravity of their crimes.

Off the back of this public fascination was spawned books (including this one!) which detailed their story, countless documentaries and even a couple of feature films. Their fame was never of any practical help to Ronnie and Reggie though. Yes, they made some money from their media enterprises – some people say they made more money than any of their criminal exploits – but you can't enjoy money behind bars.

The pair were only ever seen together again in public in 1982, when they attended the funeral of their beloved mother. Security was exceptionally tight and, in what many saw as an attempt to undermine their status and portray them as small men, Ronnie and Reggie were handcuffed to the tallest warders the prison service could find.

The pair were absent at the funeral of their father the following year. They did not request to attend because they wished to avoid the spectacle which the media turned the occasion of their mother's funeral into.

After serving ten years as a category A prisoner, Ronnie was certified insane and sent to Broadmoor secure hospital. Ronnie remained at Broadmoor until his death – from cardiac arrest – on the 17th of March 1991, aged sixty-one

Reggie went through the prison system as both a category A then B prisoner. He served his time at a variety of jails throughout England, eventually being downgraded to category C in 1997 and transferred to Wayland prison in Norfolk. He was released on compassionate grounds in 2000, after it was confirmed he was suffering from a terminal illness. Only a few weeks later, he died aged sixty-six, on the 1st of October 2000.

The Kray family (including Charlie, who died a few months before Reggie in 2000) and Frances lie buried in a graveyard in Chingford, London. It has almost become a place of pilgrimage, to which the curious and the morbid often gravitate to pay their respects to Britain's most infamous brothers....

THE END

Please See The Following Page

OTHER BOOKS by DAN SHAW:

The Great Train Robbery.

In the early hours of Thursday 8th August 1963 at rural
Cheddington in Buckinghamshire, a Travelling Post
Office train was on the final leg of its journey from
Glasgow to London. Complying with a red signal light,
the train was brought to a stop on a remote section of
track. Suddenly, and without warning, the engine was
boarded and taken over by masked men. So began
legend of the 'Great Train Robbery'....
Dan Shaw, author of 'The Krays: Their Life and Crimes'
recounts the dramatic true story of that most audacious
of crimes. Presented succinctly, from the start this book
places the reader at the very heart of the action and
gives them a bird's eye view of the roller coaster of a
story which encompasses everything from genesis of the
plan, its execution, the police hunt, capture and trial,
subsequent escapes from prison and life on the run.
It's a real life high octane thriller which will have the
reader on the edge of their seat.

The Real Bank Job

t was the most audacious crime of the 1970's; a gang of
villains tunnelled their way into the safety deposit box
vault of Lloyds Bank on Baker Street, London. The

'walkie-talkie' robbery (as it became known) was later immortalised in the hit 2008 film 'The Bank Job' starring Jason Statham.

Dan Shaw, Author of 'The Krays: Their Life and Crimes' and 'The Great Train Robbery' presents the explosive true account of one of the most daring and ingenious heists in British criminal history. It's a story packed with suspense and intrigue, near misses, and edge of the seat plot twists.
Dan Shaw has managed to cram all the drama of the real bank job into one concise yet electrifying account, taking the reader by the scruff of the neck and propelling them into the centre of what is a truly astounding story.

Dare you join the gang as they attempt the real 'Bank Job'?

Printed in Great Britain
by Amazon